PRAISE FOR RAQUEL CHALFI

"Raquel Chalfi's poems are filled with sharp intelligence, but also passion, gusto, and surprise. You never know where these poems are going, but they are carrying a fully lived life of pleasure and pain with them—and often they will sneak up on you and make you laugh. Or else make you want to dance."

— ALICIA OSTRIKER

"This is very wise poetry, insightful, often reminiscent of Wisława Szymborska—in its lucidity, its intellectualism, its new humanism . . . The range of its subject matter and the consistency of its philosophy are unique and highly impressive."

— ARIEL HIRSCHFELD

"Raquel Chalfi electrifies words that are very familiar to us, and makes us see, for the first time, what we have seen many times without seeing. She's a lyrical poet, subtle and precise, whose work radiates warmth, life, and wisdom."

— AMOS OZ

"Chalfi's poetry is complex, it cannot be defined or labeled as belonging to any particular literary trend—a multifaceted poetry, linguistically rich and daring."   — *Haaretz*

"Chalfi is an important poet. There is independence and risk-taking in her work, and she has broken through several literary fences . . . You can feel the earth shaking under your feet . . . Her poetry is unique and remarkable . . . No one writes like her."

— GABRIEL MOKED

"Chalfi tries to seize nothingness, to peel off the layers of spiritual existence . . . She spreads her broad poetic wings over all this with great momentum and unimaginable gentleness."

— *Dimui*

PRAISE FOR TSIPI KELLER'S *Poets on the Edge:*
An Anthology of Contemporary Hebrew Poetry

"... an introduction for an English-speaking audience to the wealth of contemporary poets writing in Israel today ... The careful translations are sensitive to both Hebrew cadence and English idiom. Covering a wide range of themes including love, politics, doubt, death, identity, and even poetry itself, these poems are a carefully curated collection."
— *Jewish Book World*

"This new anthology of Hebrew poetry in translation has two special strengths—tremendous depth and a personal touch ... It's clear that [Keller] has strong feelings on which poets matter, and wants to explain why they matter."
— *Jerusalem Post*

"*Poets on the Edge* deserves to be in every poetry lover's library, and should be on every Jewish bookshelf. Not since Carmi's 1981 *Penguin Book of Hebrew Verse* has a volume of such significance been published."
— *The Jewish Daily Forward*

"This comprehensive and amazing anthology is a great read best taken slowly, savoring each page of outstanding poetry. Tsipi Keller has had the patience and intelligence to select a stimulating and powerful group of poems, with accurate and very readable translations."
— SHIRLEY KAUFMAN

"*Poets on the Edge* is a true masterpiece. The translations are sensitive, wise, graceful, and insightful; the selection is rich and inviting. What a brilliant achievement!"
— MIRIYAM GLAZER

"Keller's breathtaking anthology, some twenty years in the making, shows that voices of contemporary Israeli poetry can be compellingly narrative, elegantly lyrical, elegiac, passionate, eccentric, and even phantasmagoric. Her translations convey the skepticism, wit, and energy of these poets who speak of loves and breakups, query their places in Jewish history, contemplate metaphysical questions, and paint pictures of everyday life in Israel."
— LYNN LEVIN

reality crumbs

excelsior editions

AN IMPRINT OF STATE UNIVERSITY OF NEW YORK PRESS

Reality Crumbs

SELECTED POEMS

Raquel Chalfi

TRANSLATED BY
Tsipi Keller

WITH AN AFTERWORD BY
Dan Miron

COVER ART BY DANIEL TADMON CHALFI

Published by
STATE UNIVERSITY OF NEW YORK PRESS, ALBANY

© 1975, 1979, 1986, 1990, 1995, 1999, 2004, 2007, 2009, 2010
Raquel Chalfi
Translation © 2015 Tsipi Keller

Printed in the United States of America

EXCELSIOR EDITIONS IS AN IMPRINT OF
STATE UNIVERSITY OF NEW YORK PRESS

For information, contact State University of New York Press, Albany, NY
www.sunypress.edu

Production and book design, Laurie D. Searl
Marketing, Fran Keneston

Library of Congress Cataloging-in-Publication Data

Chalfi, Rachel, author.
[Poems. Selections. English]
Reality crumbs : selected poems / Raquel Chalfi ;
translated by Tsipi Keller ; afterword by Dan Miron.
pages cm. — (Excelsior editions)
Includes index.
ISBN 978-1-4384-5741-3 (hardcover)
ISBN 978-1-4384-5742-0 (pbk.)
ISBN 978-1-4384-5743-7 (e-book)
I. Keller, Tsipi, translator. II. Title.
PJ5054.C4225A2 2015
892.41'6—dc23
2014036358

10 9 8 7 6 5 4 3 2 1

Contents

Preface   XI
Tsipi Keller

From *Underwater Poems and Other Poems* (1975)
On the Shore, Tel Aviv, Winter 1974   3
From the Songs of Crazy Dolores   4
A Brief Love   8

From *Freefall* (1979)
Traveling to Jerusalem on a Moon Night   11
Hair of Night   12
Freefall   14
The Water Queen of Jerusalem   15
Reckless Love   16
I Drew My End Near   18
For   19
Handling Pain   20
Daily Record   21
Chameleon   23
Niche   24

A Sex-Mechanic in Berkeley   25
Sitting in the Wall   26
Going Up and Down the Stairs   27
The Magical Cat   28
And the Whiteness Grew Stark   29
Optimism in an English Meadow   31

From *Chameleon or the Principle of Uncertainty* (1986)
Tutti's Seven Energy Balls   35
Voices Near the Sea   39
Poem about Sky, Stone, Sea   40
Suddenly   41
An Open Letter to Poetry Readers   42
Dissolves   44
Relationship, 2   45
I Went to Work as an Ostrich   46
Signs   48

From *Matter* (1990)
Once I Knew   53
Such Tenderness   54
A Hat's Architecture   55
Elegy for a Friend Who Lost Her Mind   56
Tale about an Inside-Out Dress   57
Bear Song   58
Parrot in My Brain   59
A Hidden Passenger   60
Blues in a Jar   61
Reality Crumbs in Café Marsand   62
Sometimes   At Noon   68
Busy   69

Eurydice 70

*(First line: And now what?) 72

From *Love of the Dragon* (1995)

The Soul or Possibly 75

A Moment in the Inner Glass 76

Birthmark 77

Cubism 78

Scanner (tr. by the poet) 79

The Love of Trees 81

Wings 83

German Boot 85

Internal Gymnastics 92

Sub-Matter 94

Three Women, Strangers, Watch Me by the Sea 95

From *A Hidden Passenger* (1999)

Organism, Chaos 99

Let Me Have a Bowl 101

Greenhouse Effect 102

The Glow of the Child 104

Pictures from a Diary 105

Space Pockets 108

Laundry 110

The Objects 112

Nearly 113

Suckling 114

From *Portrait of Father and Daughter* (2004)

To Watch Life 117

I Put Over My Head 118

I'm Sitting   119

And How You're Trying To Make Me Laugh   120

This Man   121

*(First line: When I came in here today)   123

Father Who Comes and Appears   124

From *Secret Details from the Transparent Binder* (2007)

The Cute Word-Strollers   127

More and More They Wrap   128

When Pain Becomes a Flower   129

Metaphors   130

Here   in the Hidden House   131

Ants   133

In Such a Furnace of Noon   134

So Why Don't I   136

Don't Tell Me   137

Double Exposure in the Black Forest   138

A Half-Day Off   140

Love at McDonald's   142

The Cat Frasier as a Philosophy Major   143

A Moment Tries to Catch Itself by Its Tail   144

Cinema   146

If Only I Were a Fearless Biker   147

Sixty-Five Million Years Ago   149

Short Ones   150

From the Diary of a Penguinette (tr. by the poet)   152

Mrs. Darwin (tr. by the poet)   156

From *Witches* (2009)

A Witch Bent on Healing   161

The Witch Who Did Not Cushion Her Life   162

Mutant Witch   163

Witch Breaks 164

Witch in Fact 165

Hopeful Witch 166

The Witches' Chorus 167

Monologue of the Witch Impregnated by the Devil 168

The Fat Witch's Blues 169

Witch Discusses the Color Scale 171

From *Portrait of Mother and Daughter* (2010)

Weaving 175

A Small Prayer 176

Scar Tissue 177

Ejection Seat 178

Life as an Enormous Beast 179

She 180

Back Yard 181

In the Tiny Speck 182

From the Notebook 183

Mother 184

My First Dream about You 185

The Neighborhood Cats, And Also the Birds 186

Someone Went Past 187

And Now 188

Afterword 189
Dan Miron

Acknowledgments 215

About Raquel Chalfi 217

About Tsipi Keller 220

About Dan Miron 221

Index of Titles and First Lines 223

Preface

Raquel Chalfi and I met in the early 1970s through a mutual friend, the late Tzila Binder, an artist and a poet. Tzila and I would meet every morning at Tzila's regular table at Café Capri, downstairs from her apartment on Chen Boulevard in Tel Aviv. We would sit for an hour or so and, often, friends and acquaintances would stop by for a quick exchange, or sit down and join us.

One such morning there appeared at our table a tall woman, slow-moving, like a dancer. The look in her green-gray eyes was focused, and yet conveyed long distances. I remember that she seemed exotic to me, like a bird from a different continent. Her otherworldly quality had nothing to do with dress or manner; it emanated from her face, her eyes, and from the unhurried, nearly meditative cadence of her voice. I also sensed that whatever this quality was that set her apart from us and from her surroundings, was something she tried to camouflage. This was Raquel Chalfi, recently back from her studies in the United States.

A decade or so later, when I began to work on what would become *Poets on the Edge: An Anthology of Contemporary Hebrew Poetry* (SUNY Press, 2008), Chalfi was one of the first poets I approached. During my annual visits in Tel Aviv, we would meet daily to go over the poems and the translations; when I was back in the United States, we would correspond or speak on the telephone.

᠅

Raquel Chalfi's childhood—a childhood of transitions and relocations—began in a rented room in Tel Aviv, before the family moved to a kibbutz. A couple of years later they left the kibbutz and took residence in a small apartment in a housing project in South Tel Aviv.

When she turned twelve, the family moved yet again, this time to Mexico City, where her parents served for three years as Israel's educational envoys. In addition to her high school studies and acquiring two new languages, Spanish and English, Chalfi continued her piano and dance lessons, which were her passion. Back in Israel, bits of Mexico would surface in her early poetry, notably in the cycle "From the Songs of Crazy Dolores":

> I am the child
> above whose bed
> Mexican gods laugh
>
> Seasons go by, a sun reigns
> and pyramids do not turn upside down
>
> There are many antiquities in the land of *Mejico*
> and I am the smallest among them

After her compulsory military service, working as a journalist, Chalfi moved to Jerusalem, where she studied at the Hebrew University, completing her M.A. in English literature. She was writing poetry by then, but, as yet, had made no attempt to publish it.

While a student at the university, Chalfi wrote stories and plays, winning Best Original Play Award from the National Council for Culture and the Arts. She also worked as a radio broadcaster and editor, producing documentaries, reading poetry (never her own), and discussing social and historical issues; some of the topics she raised sparked debates in the Knesset. A few years later Radio Barcelona awarded her the international documentary radio prize, Ondas, for a documentary series she produced, recording Israeli soldiers expressing their desire for peace.

She received her M.A. with honors and was soon working for Israeli television, directing documentaries which were very well received and rebroadcast over the years. Later, having won a study grant and the Shubert Playwriting Award from the University of California at Berkeley, Chalfi left for California, where her play *Contact Print* was produced by the University's drama department, and her documentary film *Matchmakers* was shown at Berkeley's Pacific Film Archive (1976). She won a scholarship from the American Film Institute and moved to Los Angeles. Her play *Felicidad* was published by *Drama and Theater* (New York, 1974).

Upon her return to Israel, Chalfi joined the Film and Television faculty at Tel Aviv University, where she taught filmmaking. Her first poetry collection, *Underwater Poems and Other Poems* (1975), and her second collection, *Freefall* (1979), appeared, drawing attention to this new and singular poetic voice. Years later, Professor Dan Miron would describe Chalfi as a poet possessed of a unique voice, already evident in her early poems, a poet who has opened "a new poetic channel, unleashing hitherto trapped energies . . . a brave and original poet, whose contribution to breaking barriers and blazing new trails is important; a pioneer laying the foundations for an alternative literary culture."

While teaching at Tel Aviv University, she continued her radio and film work. A feature script she wrote won a prize for Best Original Screenplay from the National Council for Culture and the Arts. In the early 1980s she made two experimental, underground films that won prizes from the Israel Film Institute and were screened at Israeli and international film festivals.

In time, Chalfi dedicated herself primarily to poetry, and, during the past few years, she has been engaged in conserving and publishing the work of her late mother, the sculptor and poet Miriam Chalfi Baruch; the work of her late father, the poet and playwright Shimshon Chalfi; and the work of her late uncle, the poet and actor Avraham Chalfi.

❧

Chalfi published her first collection in 1975 and has since carved for herself a niche in contemporary Hebrew poetry, digging new linguistic and rhythmic tunnels, while keeping her steady gaze on those around her, humans and animals alike. Many of her poems take place outdoors, usually in a café or on a street corner, and her locale is usually Tel Aviv. Sometimes she will travel, but not too often and not too far. Ever present in her work is the need to touch, to feel the tangible and the sensuous, often with the help of concrete physical details. An early poem, "On the Shore, Tel Aviv, Winter 1974," from her first collection, written in the aftermath of the Yom Kippur War, begins

> A crocodile cloud swallowed a cloud-cloud.
> All is clogged
> and where did the war go?
> The pier is painted yellow and red
> with the inscription: Tel Aviv.
> The drums of the depths are indifferent.
> In the sky shadowy figures
> slowly go berserk. An infinite wrestling arena
> in slow-motion takes.

One gets the sense that the poet, looking for consolation, comes to the beach, a place that is normally a source of joy for her, but this time her gloom engulfs all that she sees, painting it gray, the poet imagining "drums of the depths" even as she notes that the "pier is painted yellow and red" like a clown whose task it is to cheer up the viewer. The poem proceeds slowly, despondently, in the empty, desolate seascape. Nothing moves, except for the shadowy figures in the sky, slowly going berserk. She notices

> A lone woman, a synthetic kerchief
> on her head   what is she
> in face of a thunderstorm.

In face of wars and destruction, all Woman can do—as she has done for centuries—is remember, mourn, and try to speak:

An old woman,   her lips attempt:

He was an angel

He was an angel

For all her apparent personal calm, and her slow, deliberate speech
when you meet her, many of her poems are informed by a tension and
an agitation unique to Chalfi. The poems are often anxious, restless,
inquisitive, nearly physical in their constant, energetic search for, and
chasing after, that one element that will help them get a step closer to
grasping the mystery at their center. At the same time, they also re-
flect the maniacal, mechanized, motorized tempo of modern urban life.
While we rush on our petty, enormously important errands, always in
transit from here to there, Chalfi tells us (in "Traveling to Jerusalem on
a Moon Night") that

The window travels the clouds travel I
travel . . .
   . . .
the light travels the glass travels the galaxy travels the moon
      travels
and God
eternally
stands

Along with anxiety and restlessness, an ingredient almost always
present in Chalfi's poems is humor—subtle, usually self-deprecating,
coming from despair and futile questioning, but never malicious to,
or judgmental of, others. There is also a defining impulse to rebel
against the established order, and to expose the underlying smugness
and hypocrisies. A desire to break all boundaries and smash the so-
called conventional wisdoms, be they social, cultural, linguistic. And
finally, a need to be reckless, if only for the duration of the poem.
In her poem "Reckless Love," not only is the love reckless, but so is
the poem:

Outside   people with plastic hammers banged
each other over the head   and we drank hot chocolate.
His eyes transmitted a black madness   and I bit
into it as into a cake. The waitress came out of a Fellini movie
and asked if we wanted Hamantaschen.

. . .

It was Purim in the street.   The air was scented
with early spring.
I put lipstick on my nose and matches in my ears.
A red-nosed clown wept his childhood with him.
He was damaged
I was damaged
he traveled in me in land and sea

Sex, too, is a clash between expectations, couched in fantasy. Women somehow have a hard time getting it right, but they keep on trying. In "Tutti's Seven Energy Balls," we meet Tutti—just one of the many personas and masks Chalfi likes to try on for size in her work:

Tutti rolled her sexual energy
into a ball   and tossed it up high
in the air
(a glowing ball,   multi-colored)

Tutti's ball of sex   (multi-sexed)   rose up
to the clouds
and then
fell
on her head   with a thump

Indeed, in Raquel Chalfi's poems women often get it on the head, or even break their bones, as happens in the aforementioned "From the Songs of Crazy Dolores":

Belik is a strange man.
He wrote me a poem of love

yet refused to kiss my bare soul
under the *huppa*. It was a *huppa*
                    made of a parachute
and he jumped with it out of there
                              down,
leaving me to freefall.

Of course I arrived before him.
                    Boom.
I managed somehow
to break my bones.

Even motherhood, and the supreme joy it may bring, give rise to
anxiety and doubt. In the longish poem "Pictures from a Diary" comes
a startling moment when Chalfi, a new mother, discovers not only her
love for her child but also a phenomenon not much talked about or
admitted to:

My child
five hundred seventy nine days and nights
you sucked my milk   for you I turned myself into a warm
    whitish ball
I gathered myself around me-you every hour   daynight
    daynight
you sucked and sucked   my body gave up the hunger for
    sleep   I
became for you
a soothing fountain ...
  ...
Not to be with your child when you are with him
to feel for the first time how you close off to him
to respond to him absentmindedly   absent emotionally
    physically
not to be with him when you're with him
letting this bubbling spring   letting this being
stir around you   and you push it away calmly   you withdraw

Versatile and unpredictable, Chalfi's work—in the words of poet and critic Eli Hirsch—is a "thrilling combination of simplicity and chaos, clarity and mystery." Still, however wild, her poems are always grounded in real, everyday issues, addressing particular problems and fears that assail us mortals. Her work strongly conveys a need to be as honest as is humanly achievable, not so much for the reader's sake as for her own. If she takes on the persona of a wild biker, or of a witch, it is not merely to travel freely in the land of fancy and so taste another's life, but, more importantly, to measure the extent of her empathy. In one of her Witches poems, "The Fat Witch's Blues," she is the witch who stuffs and fattens herself as a survival strategy:

> a mouth that sucks like a tunnel
> swallowing stowing
> protecting and shielding
> so I'll be ugly   protected from love
> systematically swelling up
> so I can absorb the kick
> so I won't be good enough
> to lay

Alongside such ravenous lines come tender, lyrical moments when Chalfi slows down the pace and is simply a part of a less hectic scene, observing a beloved father ("Laundry"), or a son ("The Glow of the Child"). Yet, even in such tranquil moments of contemplation, anxiety and an awareness of death are invariably present. In the poem "Freefall," as she falls, the poet hears stones telling her that this is how it is in life:

> long ago we too dropped with a bitter wail
> look at our this-is-it-*ness*
> and learn from us
> soon you will be lying with us
> hard   dull   cold to your wants

The sound of the thud
was brief.

Since then
I lie inert.

"No one writes like her," says literary critic Gabriel Moked. A sen-
sibility apart, Chalfi is the involuntary spy, or more accurately, a "hidden
passenger," forever fascinated by the appetites and the seemingly insa-
tiable hunger of those around her. Sometimes their physicality, border-
ing on vulgarity, annoys her, but soon she is remorseful: she punishes
herself for her mean-spirited thoughts and conjures an image of herself
as an old and bitter woman:

> Find myself in Café Marsand
> humming like these old ladies
> seated at round tiny tables
> licking cream-puffs with care
> smearing with trembling hands blazing red lipstick
> on collapsed lips
> . . .
> Find myself in the large mirror   opposite
> concealing in my haughty body
> a very old   anxious lady
> bent with fear

> (from "A Hidden Passenger")

Or, in the poem "A Moment in the Inner Glass," she notices someone
she knows, but chooses to ignore her:

> Suddenly I saw an old lady
> I once knew. I wanted to go up to her and say hello
> but the swine in me

said: Don't bother, and anyhow
she won't remember. Don't bother.
This swine has overtaken
the entire inner space.
Nothing remains
in me
to fight her.

And then,   a kind of a light breeze of yearning
for something
I'm not sure what
turned my head
ever so slightly
toward her.
I saw her standing there   lost
forsaken.

Something so easily
turns beastly in me.
The inner rage
flexes its muscles.
The flesh of the soul
thickens.

For all her desire to be left alone, one senses a generosity, a need
to include and contain all of life. People, fish, trees, dogs, cats—Chalfi
takes them in, wishing to embrace the universe, its wondrous variety, its
human frivolities. Poet Alicia Ostriker, referring to Chalfi's work as "as-
tonishing," describes her poem "German Boot" as "a masterpiece of re-
alistic and comic self-mockery laced with pungent Midrash, ultimately
turning surreal, mythic, and terrifying."

A form sometimes favored by Chalfi is the long poem, stretch-
ing over a number of pages ("German Boot" is one). In "Reality
Crumbs in Café Marsand," what may have begun as a few snippets of

conversation and gossip from nearby tables soon becomes a Brechtian opera, packed with anguish and hilarity:

> —I really didn't feel like going to the funeral.
> Instead I felt like taking a swimming lesson
> but when I got to the funeral
> I saw that my boss was there
> I wanted to talk to him about my job
> the entire time I was scheming to sneak in a word
> at least about a promotion but suddenly the funeral began.

Presently, the poet herself becomes entangled in the words swirling around her and is compelled to add her voice to this incremental repetition of human grievances, comic as they may be:

> How can we live in a broken nutshell
> burning in a fire of hollow confusion
> while all around us swell gales
> of hate burning in a fire of self-love
> how can we live how can we survive
> in such a fire
> ah, I ask you
> I ask myself you myself

Also included in this collection are poems from the two volumes Chalfi published after much deliberation: *Portrait of Father and Daughter* (2004), dealing with the death of her father, and later, *Portrait of Mother and Daughter* (2010), about the death of her mother. Chalfi nursed them both during the long years of illness, and, as she explains in the preface to *Portrait of Mother and Daughter*, the notes and lines she managed to jot down became her close allies, like sisters and brothers one can "sigh with, weep with, hope for the best on their shoulders with, and grieve with." When she could, she would briefly escape to a nearby café, feeling guilty for having left a parent's sickbed. For long years, Chalfi kept these notes and poems, this diary of sorts, in the drawer until she agreed to publish them. These beautiful, private poems seesaw between hope and despair, resignation and impotent anger. I'll quote two short excerpts, one from each volume:

> Here is this man so dear to you
> lying motionless   prancing before you in a frenzy
> the whole of him made of shifting
> mosaic fragments of hope and despair and a round soft-
>   fleshed prayer
> and a sharp-toothed doubt tearing
> tearing chunks in you
>
> Here is this man
>
> And he's your father
>
>   (from "This Man")

In the poem "Back Yard," Chalfi has left her ailing mother with a care-taker and run out to a café. On the way—

> I went past the back yard of a building, with its dusty
> pine trees   straining   and the neglected shrubbery   innocent
> and the beauty hidden there.   And something stirred in me
> aching.   As if all the dreams and the lively efforts of people
> get shoved into their back yards   into
> the tool sheds   the junk piles   the garbage dumps

ॐ

If poetry is the art of compression and economy, Hebrew natural-ly lends itself to this art, thanks to its structural compactness. As in all Semitic languages, Hebrew words are formed from roots of two or three consonants by inserting vowels and by adding prefixes and suffixes to the root, indicating possession, tense, gender, and number. Because of the way these prefixes and suffixes are added, a single word in Hebrew may often require several words in English, affecting the length of the line and the overall visual poem on the page. The translator's task, therefore, is to stay as close as possible to the Hebrew syntax, while adhering to the rhythm and musicality of the line and of the poem in both languages.

A more difficult task, helped by notes, is to transmit the full resonance of certain Hebrew words and their link to the Bible and the Talmud, a link that most Hebrew speakers are aware of, as the Bible and the Talmud are taught in school and are an integral part of everyday life and speech. Still, when the poet alludes to a biblical verse, and the translator dutifully adds a note, one can only hope that the impact of the historical and emotional layers has been transmitted, as well as the wordplay.

For example: in the aforementioned "Pictures from a Diary," Chalfi begins one of the stanzas with a citation: "Bone of her self, flesh of her flesh"—an allusion to and a play on: "And Adam said, This is now bone of my bones, and flesh of my flesh: she shall be called Woman, because she was taken out of Man." (Genesis 2:23. See footnote 10.) Whereas Adam assertively declares possession of the woman, famously created from one of his ribs, Chalfi, whose baby has come out of her *self*, of her being, marvels in the lines right after the biblical allusion: "Your separateness./The astonishment: Is it from me that this wondrous creature came?" And while Adam employs the first person *(etzem m'atzmotai u'vasar m'bsari)*, Chalfi does not rush to take credit for this miracle and employs the third person *(etzem m'atzma, basar m'bsara)*.

The root here is composed of three Hebrew letters: *Ain-Tzadik-Mem*. Depending on the vowels inserted, the root becomes *etzem* (bone, and, depending on the context: object, substance, essence) or *otzem* (strength, might). And, if you add the suffix *aut* you get *atzmaut* (independence). And, as we've seen, changing the vowel and adding *a* to the root, we get *atzma*—her self. Add the prefix *m* and we get *m'atzma*—from her self.

Additionally, the Hebrew line *(etzem m'atzma, basar m'bsara)* is short, requiring four words, while the English requires eight (or seven, if we combine the *her self* into *herself*, but in this context we need the separation, for emphasis).

Such compression and resonances have benefited Hebrew poets since biblical times, and Hebrew poets have reciprocated in kind, and still do, adding to and enriching the language with new and inventive combinations, often for ironic effects. One senses a linguistic giddiness and excitement, even a recklessness, in the poetry and in the street, as all participate in the privilege of renewing and "renovating" the language. Chalfi, especially, triumphs and excels at this. Amos Oz writes: "Raquel Chalfi electrifies words that are very familiar to us, and makes us see, for the first time, what we have seen many times without seeing. She's a lyrical poet, subtle and precise, whose work radiates warmth, life, and wisdom."

Often, when I read her poems, I find myself thinking that Raquel Chalfi, in her quickness of mind and intelligence, is blessed to have Hebrew on her side. And Hebrew is blessed to have her.

From *Underwater Poems and Other Poems* (1975)

ON THE SHORE, TEL AVIV, WINTER 1974

A crocodile cloud swallowed a cloud-cloud.
All is clogged
and where did the war go?
The pier is painted yellow and red
with the inscription: Tel Aviv.
The drums of the depths are indifferent.
In the sky shadowy figures
slowly go berserk. An infinite wrestling arena
in slow-motion takes.
A crane rises above the luxury hotel
Hilton. And where did the war go.
A crocodile cloud swallowed a cloud-cloud. Where
did the war go. Up in the depths
soft clouds make love to planes.
The air fills the lungs
with spiky salt and laughter.
The sun, a fading photograph.
Shorebirds grayly peck the sand.
The sea—its muscles groan.
A lone woman, a synthetic kerchief
on her head   what is she
in face of a thunderstorm.
The diving board, too, is painted orange.

An old woman,   her lips attempt:

> He was an angel
> He was an angel

FROM THE SONGS OF CRAZY DOLORES

1.

I am the child
above whose bed
Mexican gods laugh

Seasons go by, a sun reigns
and pyramids do not turn upside down

There are many antiquities in the land of *Mejico*
and I am the smallest among them

2.

I love Beli-Belik-Boom
(once I called him Le-Le-Le)
and I'll always love Le-Le-Le.
But Belik does not understand
what love is.

Belik is a strange man.
He wrote me a poem of love
yet refused to kiss my bare soul
under the *huppa**. It was a *huppa*
                    made of a parachute
and he jumped with it out of there
                              down,
leaving me to freefall.

Of course I arrived before him.
                    Boom.

---

* The wedding canopy.

I managed somehow
to break my bones.
And I have a few memories left.

When I was broken
and a memory only
Belik would kiss me on my cheek (Le-Le-Le)
every evening.
Later he swapped me
for a cat.
When he photographed me
he would photograph me in double
exposure.
Somehow I managed to appear in the picture.
Boom.

3.
I am made of glass
and my father is a glazier
I tell you I'm as
transparent as a yogurt jar
without the yogurt
try to look through me   just try
and you'll see that you can see everything
lean your head on me   children
and your noses will be squashed flat
and your mouths will be pulled
like a down-in-the-mouth blowfish
take a look inside me I'm transparent
absolutely
I am made of glass
because my daddy is a glazier
and my mother dons a tulle dress
take a look children take a look

it will do you good
only be a little cautious please
yesterday someone looked through me too hard
and saw as far as the Bali islands
and he rode a blue whale   in the Bali islands
and then my glass broke
into a zillion shards
and I was pricked and pricked and pricked
and I was all glass glass
in a zillion red puddles

4.
Dolores jumps rope
Dolores plays hopscotch

She looks into a kaleidoscope
tube   builds
broken tunnels in a dream
Dolores lives her life backward
swings on a rusty groaning gate
looks for puppies to adopt
dead chicks to revive
diamonds buried in trashcans
in order to help refugees
hiding in a tunnel under
Keren Hakayemet Boulevard*
on the other side of the world

Dolores jumps rope
always jumps rope
to the other side of the world

---

* Boulevard in Tel Aviv named for the Jewish National Fund.

5.

I am Dolores-not-Dolores
I am in the dream of some god

It seems to me that my life is a life
but really it is only
a particle in the dream
of a sleeping god
who dreams me with love

Dolores-not-Dolores

I have to pinch myself hard
because the hour when images switch in his brain
is near

Yes Dolores no Dolores yes Dolores no
Dolores birds Dolores sea Dolores
a loose shoelace Dolores a broken blue glass a milky
way bathing a world
a white horse lost in the plain
tunnels inside time
time going backward
a snake shedding its skin a mobile of broken galaxies
suspended on fine transparent fiber

I have to pinch myself hard
because the hour when images switch in his brain is near
I must watch myself so I don't sink
in a dream
when he dumps me from his brain
like a crumb dropping
from indolent fingers

A Brief Love

Slices slices silence cut
into us

He took me from the noise
and time became a summer of grace
between killings
and I reached my hand   and he came like a rain of grace
and on Mount Zion the darkness was thick
and the little light in the churchyard was frail   frail
and I reached my hand   and he fell into me in despair
    despair
and later he led me by the hand
like the sighted lead the blind
and we saw so much so much
it was possible to touch the very roots of things
and we saw until our eyes refused to retain
two beautiful weeks
between wars
do you know what it means two full innocent weeks
between death and death
one cannot ask for more and were we to ask for more
it would have been a kind of arrogance

It was a cruel beauty

And such a silence
on the altar*

---

* Alludes to the covenant God made with Abram (Genesis 15:18).

From *Freefall* (1979)

Traveling to Jerusalem on a Moon Night

The window travels the clouds travel I
travel the road travels the moon travels the trees travel the pane
travels the moon travels the travelers travel
the earth travels the mountains travel the planet travels the
    thoughts travel
the time travels
the light travels the glass travels the galaxy travels the moon
    travels
and God
eternally
stands

HAIR OF NIGHT

To weave the locks of darkness
a thick braid on the downy nape
of the earth
to mold with moist hands
the clay of dark craving
tremor-plaited trees
coiled branches of devotion
and a broad meadow
waiting in vain

Night combs its long hair like a woman
seated at her window at night

Night hungry runs barefoot through the streets
weeds spread rumors about it

Night begets day what will day bring
night its dreams undone
breaks the heart of a city
tears a street apart
how I wish to dye
the hair of night
a startling orange

How we wished for a blaze to spread in the twigs   twigs as
    blaze
to sweep the trail of excess words
to leave a clear polished dance floor for thick dense emotions
to spin into a dance into a giant ball

How I wished for the great night's hair
to wrap around me like snakes   but warm

Such naked truth even the down of dusk
stiffens
the mind's shutters knock violently
a blow of darkness
rescues a night
whose hairs got all tangled up

Dreams,   the heart's sweat,
on night's taut skin
its hair pulled back   its temples damp
secretions of dreams drop from it
drip
drop
cool
salty

Such an old night
its chimes still clear

And we
crawl on its belly
and it welcomes us inside
like a mad satyr who's fallen asleep
                              blissfully

FREEFALL

And until the sound of my falling plea was heard
I would eagerly fall
through the sky's chimneys
toward the land of my desires

Falling falling   the floating angels wailed
this is how the wishes drop   from
the bitter gravitational pull   this is how it is in life
this is it   said the stones lying inert
on the ground since time immemorial
long ago we too dropped with a bitter wail
look at our this-is-it-*ness*
and learn from us
soon you will be lying with us
hard   dull   cold to your wants

The sound of the thud
was brief.

Since then
I lie inert.

The Water Queen of Jerusalem

The Water Queen of Jerusalem
dived into history

History was hard and she grew fins
she had no air   and she schemed
gills   rowing and rowing through memory

The Water Queen of Jerusalem has
a bathing suit made of Yiddish
the Water Queen of Jerusalem wallows on a stone beach in
     Ladino
fearing the rise of water levels in Arabic
the Water Queen of Jerusalem has no
sea in Jerusalem
she has a history
Jewish
and she   holds
holds   her head
above water

RECKLESS LOVE

blues

I was a little reckless
he was a little reckless
in a cheap café on the eve of Purim
everyone around us with the face to the TV
up on the wall.
He broadcast to me on a high frequency.   I wanted
to broadcast low-low but it came out
high.   I was a little reckless he was a little
reckless. My hair was unruly his hair was unruly
my past was undone his past was marred
he had a nervous tick in his hand and I chain-smoked
his dark face twisted in a child's smile
in my face raced electric currents
we were reckless and we knew we wouldn't
come out clean.

Outside   people with plastic hammers banged
each other over the head   and we drank hot chocolate.
His eyes transmitted a black madness   and I bit
into it as into a cake. The waitress came out of a Fellini movie
and asked if we wanted Hamantaschen.

He talked about epilepsy. I about paranoia.
It was the eve of Purim. Two clowns showed us some tricks.
We were like children when a large ship
blares   and leaves them behind.

Later,   in the park,   Your skin is like velvet.
Later,   in the park,   Go home,   or your wife will cuss you out.
Later   later   later   I was pure and beautiful.

16

It was Purim in the street.   The air was scented
with early spring.
I put lipstick on my nose and matches in my ears.
A red-nosed clown wept his childhood with him.
He was damaged
I was damaged
he traveled in me in land and sea
but he was reckless   and I was reckless
he spoke of convulsions   I of conclusions
he called for help   I called for help
he spoke of silence   and I agreed with him about everything.

What a thing it was
a great madness.
We were like two kids   when a large ship blares
and leaves them
far behind
in the sand

I Drew My End Near

I drew my end near
and it came near

A couple of cats sat in the tree like calm fruit
I called my end to come near   and it lingered on the street
    corner
one cat leapt and sat on my shoulder
I stroked the animal   but my hand hastened to stroke the
    blood
flowing in my end

My end is soft,   I know,   and patient,
I wanted so to rub against it
be warm at its side
like an old contented woman   next to her old man

For

For it is as if
you chose to die to
preserve your shadow

The flicker of light that is present and vanishes
at once
the open warm night
that is already sinking
in the sludge of lost winters

Things I have loved
are spread like a stain of oil upon
heavy water

Handling Pain

The pain comes
after the inner image

First a dull pain
in the senses which have no words

Later I project for myself
images of future painful states
or of the past or of other times   later
on comes the pain the senses can handle and the words too
express it as pain

Whoever watches me at this moment sitting cross-legged
may think I'm deep in Tibetan meditation

DAILY RECORD

I put on Bach's Cantata 87
and my spirit soared free.
Yet it lasted only a moment.
On the windowsill, to the right, crystal stones—
hard gleaming forms, a world within a world.
They stand opaque before me, completely opaque.
Behind them a glass pane stands between me
and South Jerusalem and I am not
in South Jerusalem.
Life flows at the fringes of life.
I am in the music and the music is in me
the stones come in me,   my lover, who has placed them here,
Jerusalem in me
I am in me
but by the time I had finished writing "I"
I was no longer in me   only the words only the words
remained like stone-weights at my feet.
So it flows,   life,   flows at the fringes of life.
Yesterday, an evening with Joe, Jean-Claude, Shami, Karen.
I was more in me   more in them
I wove experimental cobwebs
over the ever-present abyss
my body filling up with me.
These are people I love because they help me
love myself.
The Cantata continues, without me.   It doesn't need me
but I,   I am hungry
for me,   longing for something that is more me.
So life flows at the fringes of life.
Jean-Claude, on the stone path, at night, in the stillness,
said that Buddhism is becoming more and more important in
    his life.
It grows in him and grows.

I envied him so much. I could have devoured him
for envy. I wanted his blood to come in my blood,
I wanted to become like him. I told him that in me
nothing grows. And that which does grow for moments
dissolves into the void.

He told me in a clear and enlightened voice
that even the knowledge of nothing is something.
I was not inside the nothing when he spoke
about the feeling of nothing inside me.
Later, I'm undone again, filament after filament,
and again aspire for myself
with desperate hunger.

Now I'm alone.
The crystals to the right, the Cantata in the back,
my friends distant,   downstairs,
darkness ahead,   to the left a faint light.
What a rhymed finale,   the void held tight
with one thing leading to another, orderly.
All right, let it be.   Another day.
Who was it who said: There's another world
and it dwells within this one.

CHAMELEON

Quivering stripes in a drugged dream
of a chameleon
your lies are of spectacular colors
lavenders and blues sucked into the shadows

They are lies and they are not
transparent
a lie cannot be transparent
let no one tell me that a lie is transparent
because every lie has its own flesh tone and tremor
and every lie assembles around itself
a small concrete world
of a living truth

NICHE

My bodysoul
and your bodysoul
make out in a niche in the wall.

Nerves that have lost their transparency   that have become
     entangled
spy on us like hostile strangers
from the trenches they've burrowed into
exchanging information in foreign tongues.
White   blue   yellow particles
float farther away
in Klee's paintings   on a different wall.
Meantime   our bodiesouls
with their hands and feet
wave red and white flags to one another
and resume making out in a niche
in the wall.

A SEX-MECHANIC IN BERKELEY

*I am a sex-mechanic**
says the yellow boy, his smile as pure as wax,
a boy-girl golden specks dot his face
he's besotted with the world loves everyone
women men beasts machines above all roaring machines,
says gilded she-boy golden specks plastered on his cheeks
a sex-mechanic fixing things installing greasing restoring
    machinery
a multi-tasked sex-mechanic skinny and yellow,   angel eyes
gilded with fluttering lashes,   a small dreamy love mechanic
sits in a bar named The Haven, a warmish greenish haven
with a jolly jukebox that plays *Disco Baby*.
In need of repair I sit facing him during long nights
that shift my roots into the depths of days
and seas that separate me from my habitual continent.
I sit in complete disrepair
dim gold in my used heart   I sit
gliding over my spare parts
small and in need of repair facing a sex-mechanic
a lost broken fixer in the vastness
of this sex garage
in the bowels of an outermost town
beyond the outermost border

---

* Italics: English in the original.

SITTING IN THE WALL

The wall has a mouse   the mouse has ears
the wall has ears
Gavriela has a heart the heart has a crack
soon we will patch it up for her

The mouse in the wall sits and weeps recalling its youth
you toss it some cheese   but it nibbles
bitter nostalgia

Now the three of us sit like she-mouse and mouse
and one despondent she-mouse
sitting in the wall
and the wall doesn't know
what's going on
in our three
hearts

GOING UP AND DOWN THE STAIRS

She teaches me not to be ashamed
of the chemistry of minutes   it's not a holy alchemy
it's a raw chemistry one can write poems about
she makes things with it
going up and down the stairs of her consciousness with the
    trailing train
of the useless poetry dress
she takes the emergency exit stairs
you'd think she's walking on a flat road, blowing words.
Others will not reach for her steep railing,
I will reach for her steep railing so she won't slip
and will glide down on it
like a totally
demented girl

The Magical Cat

The magical cat
the magical cat
slowly weaves a soul
cool cautious thread by thread his quiver is woven
he recalls his many lives carries in his belly
memories of diverse cat civilizations it is difficult for him
for the magical cat to carry so much
memory the mass of memory is heavy dense
it contracts like a black star into a void-
pit from which leaps the leopard of his destiny
the magical cat walks upon a quiet ceiling
his eyes shine an attempt to comprehend the in-
comprehensible his blue fur permeates the world
the magical cat a pure magus
a clean force
his eyes flow in a fine stream of consciousness
dreaming to comprehend what it means to be a man

The magical cat bounds magically toward
a higher level of being
his body surrenders to its obvious authority
the cat surrenders to the magical master in him
the cat is master to his cat
perched on a window dozing in a magical sun
his body quivers a lucid consciousness attempting
to become more and more lucid
suddenly he says
Miau

AND THE WHITENESS GREW STARK

He went.
And I went.
And a growing white distance went
and opened
and the whiteness went stark
went and stretched.
I could have called after him
he could have called after me
but his name went and grounded itself
on the tip of my tongue.
He went.   Or maybe I went.
And a space   a large   quiet space
went and spread out between us
growing more and more comfortable
like a tired wanderer   on a white bed.
I went   he went
and air   pallid air
and guileless
went and spread between us
with the speed of light   light
growing and spreading.

He could have called me. Yes   he could have
but the word that was the thread I was connected to
fell from his fingers
and the thread went and wandered   becoming entangled.
I went   he went.
The air between us multiplied like a plague.
He went.   I went.   More and more
it was hard to feel the fingertips   the tip
of the tongue   the tip of the thread was impossible
to find   in the knot

that went and grew   went and grew mightily   went and grew
    dark
like a mountain where a myriad of shadowy satyrs lie faint
after an orgy.
He went.   Now he's not even
a dot on the horizon.
And only the empty air   goes and grows heavy   goes and
shuts.

Optimism in an English Meadow

A sun hesitates to set on an English meadow
and in my own greens a sun erupts in a cosmic *hora* dance
inebriated after a sip of ale in the nearby pub.
A herd of cows in a slanting light   mottled and good-looking
pretty in white speckles radiating a spiritual sheen
while the train sings in a reserved English glee.
At this hour   during such a journey   who considers
the fate of these cows.
On this optimistic train   traversing a British meadow
as if slicing through a loaf of rye bread from Lindy's bakery,
the Jew from Golders Green, even I am unable
to think about misfortunes.   At this moment it seems to me
that the world is delicious like a breakfast pudding in London
and I intend to taste it and go out on a conquering
cultural tour of all the colonies.
The sun slants further   and the glow lessens
toward a gray mooing.   Soon my heights
will drop somewhat.

I'd better hurry and set out on a world-conquering adventure
and if not that   then cuddle up in the orange sleeping-car
with one lover, at least

From *Chameleon*
or the Principle of Uncertainty (1986)

Tutti's Seven Energy Balls

1.
Tutti rolled her sexual energy
into a ball   and tossed it up high
in the air
(a glowing ball,   multi-colored)

Tutti's ball of sex   (multi-sexed)   rose up
to the clouds
and then
fell
on her head   with a thump

2.
Zutti settled her accounts with the world.
In conversations between herself and herself she took courage
and yelled at Dutti,   mocked Jutti,   and even
harassed the boss,   Sutti.

Then she realized it was a waste of energy.
She kneaded all into a giant ball
lifted it up with might
and hurled it
to the floor.

The ball bounced back from the floor
and hit her in the belly   brazenly.

3.
Her longings for faraway John
Shutti blew into a balloon.   She puffed into it
more
and more
pining and fe-

male longings.   Afterward she tapped
the balloon lightly with her fingertips.

The balloon took off,
bewitched,   up to the treetops.
One treetop
held it tight   and Shutti's
balloon of longing sat on it
for good.*

4.
Her erratic qualms
her pounding   worn-out dialectics
her doubts treading on eggshells
her whitish diffidence
Yutti turned into
a ping pong ball.

Yes ping
no pong

5.
The hard knocks on the heads
of the insolent internal kids
the internal blows
the self-slaps on the cheek
the fists of the internal cop   raining down
the whacks of conflicts conflicting
so much inside her   (to the extent that they turn
everything yellow inside her
into an omelet)
Hutti turned into   a racket.

---

* In Hebrew, balloon is masculine, treetop feminine.

And yet a white elegant sport
remained beyond her reach.

6.

Butti's weighty subconscious baggage
the accretion of deep masses that had yet to emerge
even in a dream (Kutti's)
grew little by little into
a huge iron ball.

And who can repel
an iron ball
inside such an internal space?

7.

Once   in a rare long-short moment
something   gathered inside Tutti
into a bubble
into some kind of vacuum   transparent   roundish
that began a hollow dance inside her
a transparent vacuum
a radiant vacuum inside her

But presently
the bubble
ascended
unseen   and seeing
dancing above Tutti's head
a gentle motionless dance
getting farther
farther   away
from her

into
the ball
of the large vacuum

The ball
of the large vacuum

The ball of the large vacuum

VOICES NEAR THE SEA

In the foreground
a Glenn Miller album   the sizzle
of steaks on the grill   electronic sounds   the tick-
tick of the calculating machine   I can't   I
can I have a hot sandwich please
when I knew him   when I knew her
noise-noise at the steak-bar

In the inner backdrop
noise inside my head   a minor roiling
inside the roiling   a wild gruel   and fears
with cinnamon from some brown dream

In the back backdrop
but in front   beyond the glass
the rolled-up silence   the great poetry   of the round sea
which the pen cannot contain
and which I cannot contain
as with all other
round things

Poem about Sky, Stone, Sea

1 I cannot touch the sky
   even if my brain tells me   feel the sky

2 The large sea is a small infinity
   wet and salty
   and I can touch it with my tongue

3 The sky is a concept with color

4 Even the sleeping stones speak
   a Gregorian chant
   even the flies dance
   following some cosmic law
   but the sky
   is too
   empty

5 I look at the sea   perceive in it
   the depth of a white concept
   turning into a blue
   of want

6 In one of the stone's transfigurations
   lovers will be lying on it
   I cannot touch the sky
   the minds of fish are hungry

SUDDENLY

Suddenly I'm light suddenly I'm heavy
suddenly I'm round suddenly I'm sharp
suddenly I'm pretty suddenly I'm hideous
suddenly I'm open suddenly I'm clogged
suddenly I'm honest suddenly I'm crooked
suddenly I'm fat suddenly I'm skinny
suddenly I'm a doer suddenly I'm a dreamer
suddenly I love suddenly I don't love
suddenly I abstain suddenly I sleep around
suddenly I'm like this and suddenly I'm like that
suddenly I am I suddenly I
am not

An Open Letter to Poetry Readers

The brain receives ten million bits per second
but transmits only two or three to consciousness.
Wise brother, big and cautious, the brain. Keeps his
little sister from going mad.
I could have written about the pastry about life about my
        beau
I could have made soaring explosive metaphors
I could have had stormy love affairs with objects   words
and reported them to the world via the AP Poetry
        Correspondent

I don't want to.
I can't. I can't want to.
The brain receives ten million bits per second
but transmits only two or three. He loves
his little sister,   keeps her well-guarded
from madness.

You want me to write about the leaf,   the quivering green
        bed,
and about a feeling that can be named ("yearning," etc.), but
        is the chamber
where minuscule currents transpire
within the great pandemonium.
You want me to exhibit my profile   the contours of my body
but not the roar of boiling archeological layers
not the stirrings of the brief
moment
where I am this one I facing that other I.   But dear poetry
        readers,
you'd better remember that
every bit travels ten million sound-light waves
and its particles, infinitesimal photons impossible to imagine

and even tinier quarks,
explode in a lethal terrorist attack.
(On this another AP correspondent will report.)
And so what can be written about such
particles that you cannot perceive
not even when equipped and armed
with a microscope

Dissolves*

Afterward
we are a different thing

Time passes   a sheet breathes   a light
becomes accustomed to itself   darkness—to us
a world becomes round
around us   and we become a neat sandwich

Afterward   sleep comes between us
and we are warm slices
the spirit touches   the body turns unto itself
and the air of dreams connects us

Another dream.   Another time.   Another light.
From body distances   we swim one toward the other
to come together again
in our eternal-ephemeral
togetherness

---

* In film editing: a superimposition of a fade-out into a fade-in. (Author's note.)

RELATIONSHIP, 2

We played at falling   and fell
a cautious fall into the pit
of the bluish-whitish-furtive hue of tentative
love

Later
alchemy made use of myour body
the colors intensified toward red
we devoured each and one another
the body swallowed the soul the soul the body

Descartes dissolved like wax

I Went to Work as an Ostrich

blues

I went to the zoo to work as an ostrich
they said: You have no qualifications to work as an ostrich
you have too many eyes and not enough sand
get it out of your head you could ever make it as an ostrich

How much sand how much sand do I need
to see everything to see everything I need
and I also need an income
to work how sweet to work as an ostrich   I'm even
willing to take it on as a hobby   volunteer as an ostrich
but please just let me
work as an ostrich

> Don't you get it?   You run run like some giant bird
> lopped from the sand of oblivion
> your head too should be lopped,   don't you get it?

I'm even willing just to pretend I'm an ostrich!
But what does it matter if I'm willing if they won't
let me be an ostrich?

> Your neck is too erect
> they tell me at the zoological employment agency
> your body is too impudent your stare too naked
> says the zoo's social worker
> don't you get it that until you've turned over in the
> turnover
> until you've turned your skin twisted your neck buried
> your head
> you have no chance as an ostrich worker?!

Maybe, at least, I'll wear a dress of ostrich feathers
it's so sensual   so sensuous

Nonsense!   It's not a matter of feathers, they scream at
me.
It's a matter of commonsense!
Of sand and commonsense!!

SIGNS

*

Nothing remains but the kingdom of articulated
signs
to stick to them while a moment roils in liquid chaos

Nothing remains but the bones of withered words
hold onto them hold on tight
in the amusement park of glittering
soap bubbles

Hold onto them hold on tight
you have no other bones

*

The river pukes itself incessantly
the stones make you stumble   and stumble in turn
the warm body schemes
the air plots evil
the world shuts like an unyielding hand fan
the battle for survival
bares two evil fangs

*

Dogs are set loose at night
leashes removed   muzzles sniff in despair
here and there
wild dogs desperately seeking
truth

*

A summer borrowed from winter

At the window a conflicted woman studies palmistry

A hand whose fate is written in it
practices swimming strokes in high tide
the air sweltering in a borrowed sun

*

To travel like a train in a smooth tunnel
to travel like a person in a train in a smooth tunnel
to switch emotional trains
to switch consciousness cars
to switch soft
stops

From *Matter* (1990)

ONCE I KNEW

Once I knew:
Prayer is a sound
aligned
traveling the universe

This knowledge—what is it to me?

In the universe travels a sound
I couldn't hear
I wished to touch it
with a sound of my being
which I couldn't align

Now   as I try
I'm like a dull   wooden table
trying to pray

SUCH TENDERNESS

Such tenderness in our body
as it abandons us
slowly
reluctant to hurt us
with a sudden jolt.
Gradually   wistfully
like a half-sleeping beauty
it weaves for us
tiny wrinkles of light and wisdom—
no earthquake cracks
but an airy network of anxiety lines.
How kind of our body
that it doesn't change our face
all at once
that it doesn't break our bones
with one blow

No,   cautiously
like a pale moon bathing us with its glow
it illumines us
with a network of sad nerves
folds our skin in the corners
hardens our spinal cord
so we can withstand it all

Such beauty   such tenderness
in our body that gradually betrays us
politely prepares us
tells us in whispers
bit-by-bit   hour-by-hour
that it is   leaving

A Hat's Architecture

There's an ascending line
in the hat of a nun

Clean and optimistic
there's something of the church in it
something of the pointed
spiritual steeple
and something as well
of the whimsical
windmill

When she takes another step
you notice
in the air
that its hard lines
are cast in motion
like the figures of plague escapees
in open
fields

Elegy for a Friend Who Lost Her Mind

You were a field of poppies breaking
under the weight of the tar of madness
I watched you go mad under its weight—
a glowing insect
under a voracious beast in the dark

I watched the warm beast pervade your body
I watched you get crushed inside and out
the muscles of your face trying to escape
the truth you know
about yourself
you're suddenly mad suddenly
and there's no escape

I watched your body   freeze
not in the hot tar of madness
frozen
in the basalt of the sane   cold fear
and in your heart the blazing heart of lava
in the black heart of frozen basalt

A girl who wishes to be good even in the face of the terrible
    dybbuk
clinging to your flesh

My friend   my body is crushed in your ache
my heart consumed in your Jobian hurt
and the sights the sights haunt me mad

Tale about an Inside-Out Dress

The inner sea was dense
sharks of possibilities cruised
left and right
a mad train-rush struggled against heavy waters
cars of refusal knocking upon refusal

Speeding through the streets of the sea
turned to a crawl in a black tunnel
ambulance sirens pierced the agony
of the masses swimming indolently breathlessly
the failed attempts to obtain permission from a sullen
    obstinate world
turned to adamant tom-tom drumming

All at once
in the middle of the failing drowning race
I noticed the rough seams
of my inside-out
dress

The streets ticked in an underwater
time bomb

The entire inner lining
was turned out

I stood there
at the intersection of black water
under the weight of the sea
to take off my dress
turn it
right side out

Bear Song

Good night my love
you're my thick blanket all around
you're my dense blood
lying in wait at the portal of whims   lover
mine   a large bear loveable lost
in me in me getting lost
and I too in you getting lost
bear and she-bear like us so brown
the lonesomeness of bears is not lonesome
a gentle brownwarm bear-hug
holding tight we'll sleep in the good
night a beautiful night a good night
some say love

PARROT IN MY BRAIN

There's a parrot in my brain
that doesn't know he's in a cage
he thinks his colors are
freedom
that his words are
philosophical breakthroughs

Parrot doesn't know he's a parrot
thinks he's a primordial bird
primordial of worthy plumage
thinks he's a pterosaur

Possibly thinks that he
is me

A Hidden Passenger

Find myself in Café Marsand
humming like these old ladies
seated at round tiny tables
licking creampuffs with care
smearing with trembling hands blazing red lipstick
on collapsed lips

Find myself sipping whipped coffee with an eager mouth
dispatching the last of my senses
to hold onto the pleasure
before I drown

Find myself in the large mirror   opposite
concealing in my haughty body
a very old   anxious lady
bent with fear
her heart beating beating

A hidden passenger

BLUES IN A JAR

Now it's better
now the troubles are in a jar
with a twist-on cap.
Now it's better
the shadows don't leap
the abyss is buttoned up
the mouth shut
the fist tight
the air tart
but all is held with a cement clip
all is utterly safe.
You can see the horrors twitch
inside the round glass
under the screwed-on cap
and it is simply a delight.
You may sprawl on your back
and observe with interest
this large jar
for it cannot
be unscrewed.
Now it's better.
Now everything is in a jar
with a twist-on cap.

Reality Crumbs in Café Marsand

Voices

—Some people feel pressure in the ears
if someone rolls down the car window
it's like they're climbing up
the Himalayas.
Go tell it to the doctor.
Tumbalaya.

—Torn bodies in a framed picture
body parts under
the glass of the frame.
Pain trapped in a righteous painting.
Go tell it to the Artists' Guild.
Tumbalaya.

—Look, look
how this great dark-brown dog
with the tourist and her crimson cake-nose
drips blood from his hairy member. Look, look,
a violent man enters and says: That hotel
sucks. Not even half a star.
Tumba-tumba Tumba-laya.

It's hard for me to write letters
especially to people I feel close to.
All words are essentially
avoidance.
A kind of dance going round-round
saying:
Don't touch me. Me, myself.
Go tell it to the Writers' Guild.

Have you ever noticed
the patience of plants.
The ancient knowledge
of old trees.
—What are you talking about? Have you lost it?
—And to think that flowers don't have the right to vote!
—Go tell it to the National Voting Committee!

—I told her I had no desire to bang her.
But she said: One may be revived by a kiss.
Go tell it to the Union of the Horny.
Tumba-ba.

—You crave his boot like a dog craves a thrashing.
—And you, you crave her like a butterfly craves a pin.

It is hard to for me write letters, especially to people I feel
     close to,
that's what I wrote him
because I felt
that all the words
are a passion to touch
a passion that knows not
what to do with itself
I wrote him
and he never bothered to reply.

—I really didn't feel like going to the funeral.
Instead I felt like taking a swimming lesson
but when I got to the funeral
I saw that my boss was there
I wanted to talk to him about my job
the entire time I was scheming to sneak in a word
at least about a promotion but suddenly the funeral began.

Go tell it to the widow.
Tumba-tumba-tumnana.

—Happiness is within you
at your fingertips really
just make room for it
a tiny corner
as if for a pin.
Tell it tell it to yourselves
Tum-baka.

Half a star hangs above the Himalayas
and a tourist with a pink cake-nose twirls round-
round with a dog
don't touch me don't touch me
open a window at the funeral,   and I feel pressure down to
      my hair ends
and who can I write letters to, do I even have someone to
      write letters to
and only the old trees know and they don't say
where's the butterfly   where's my butterfly   where's the
      butterfly within
do touch touch touch me, me myself
and how the world would have looked if only flowers had the
      right to vote
touch stroke but do not clip does a butterfly need a boot
Tumbalaya.

What pressure what pressure in the ears,   in the soul
how thin the air in the Himalayas
go tell it to the Doctors' Union
they strike during the day, swim in the evening and kill at
      night
go tell it to the bigheaded doctors
what it feels like to bleed like a dog
go suggest it to the Doctors' Union

to become for two hours a day and two hours at night
ailing members of the National Healthcare System
go tell it to the Psychologists' Union who are psychologists by
    day
and psychos by night
go tell yourselves, go tell me, no, don't tell
Tumbalaya.

How can we live in a broken nutshell
burning in a fire of hollow confusion
while all around us swell gales
of hate burning in a fire of self-love
how can we live how can we survive
in such a fire
ah, I ask you
I ask myself you myself
go tell it to the Union of Nutshell Sailors
who eat nuts
while they're being devoured
Tum-go Tum-go Payla.

The particles of confusion that contain us all
that creep in my head in your heads
frightened of themselves
they gang up with violent street gangs
of solid essence.
But even the solid
is essentially
a void
a large empty void

—And how will I sail in the void
how will I hold onto the void
quick, fill my belly
with stones
Tumboo-tumboo-boo.

—You must establish a hierarchy
of aches
you must make a selection
of fears
you must grow a thick skin
like one grows flowers in the garden
says the kindly lady
and I see
a field of nerve stems
bearing in their crowns
blistering sores
and with a small vaporizer I spray over them
a white soporific tonic.
Tum-tum-tum.

Let's say I'll learn to put a few of the flowers to sleep
does it mean there
are no flowers?

You connect to others because of want
or an abundance
that knows not what to do with itself.
Are we nurtured by want
is want nurtured by us
and where does abundance hide
and what is its wondrous sound

Abundance knows not where to go
it seeks palms, to be poured into them,
it suddenly dawns on me
and in order to plug
the hole that has opened with the thought

I bite
into another cheese cake
a slice that's half-hollow, half-bewitched
half-full
with self-love
in Café Marsand
Tum-balaga Tum-balaga
Tum. Ah.

Sometimes At Noon

Sometimes   at noon
I try to befuddle my senses
how I wish then   so much
not to feel the years lustily nibbling at me
like a green algae sea
and only feel in my hands the weight of male stares
how I wish then to crawl in the warm sands like a beast in the
    field

How I would be cavorting then inside of me
and not be singing a poem
such as this

BUSY

I'm busy I'm busy
trying to dial myself but always
a busy signal
someone's
trying to reach me
but I'm busy I don't hear
only he hears my busy
signal as I'm busy and ring busy
busy busy busy
even if God dials my number
I'll be busy

EURYDICE*

A hand in a dark silk glove
will lead you far away from here.
A woman—her inside black
her ugliness deeper than beauty—
will take your soul.
The screech of the crow
a slice of lightning
a wall of water
a broken rock
will herald her arrival.
Go with her
toward
the other side
of the looking glass

In order to break from the valley of death
it is required
that a bewitching name
like a wave—
Eurydice—
will be murmured
in a drawn-out whimper
supplicating

In order to break
Orpheus will wear earth gloves
will split open the heart of the looking glass
and with the slowness of a silk parachute
will row in a netherworld of spirits and mirrors
where he would love death
unto death

---

* After Jean Cocteau's film *Orpheus*. (Author's note.)

70

Later
he will sing in a drawn-out whimper:
To die is to return.
Loneliness is a looking glass.

And again:
Loneliness is a looking glass
to die
is to return

*

And now what?   Write another poem?
Shut an eye to the black abyss
and stifle from within the barks
of truth from around the corner
shrieking "hau! hau!"?
For words of incantation have not the power
for the magic tune has not the power
to lull the dark hairy demons
for the layer of pink powder has not the power
to cover the cracks of horror
peeping from below,   making obscene gestures

For you don't intend to hide, giggling, behind
the apron of words,
rubbing against their large soft bellies,
and for how long will you be deceiving, for how long won't
    you admit
how useless is this broken clunky magic lantern
in the face of death

From *Love of the Dragon* (1995)

The Soul or Possibly

The soul or possibly non-soul but this soft matter
this spirit pouring from me   from my drained   unfocused
body   I don't feel the lines
of its bones   I don't feel its contours
the meeting of its skin with the air   the light   the wind
ugh!   The soul or something like it overflowing its
      boundaries
and needlessly spilling
on this marble tabletop in the restaurant
without even spicing up
the salad dressing

A Moment in the Inner Glass

Suddenly I saw an old lady
I once knew. I wanted to go up to her and say hello
but the swine in me
said: Don't bother, and anyhow
she won't remember. Don't bother.
This swine has overtaken
the entire inner space.
Nothing remains
in me
to fight her.

And then,   a kind of a light breeze of yearning
for something
I'm not sure what
turned my head
ever so slightly
toward her.
I saw her standing there   lost
forsaken.

Something so easily
turns beastly in me.
The inner rage
flexes its muscles.
The flesh of the soul
thickens.

BIRTHMARK

I have a birthmark
no one can see

During quiet moments   when only
I and my body are in the room
I remove its veil
look at it
bend to kiss it

One night I called its name all night   and it
didn't come to me
it had left me to my chaste body
flew in sleep-travel to other bodies
rubbing against them   whispering whispers in their skins
only to explain to them the meaning
of birthmark

All night I called its name

Morning it came back to me   loyal
and sat at the foot of the bed.
As soon as my body opened
it jumped on it with a warm rough tongue

At times I wish that it won't return
but later I understand
that this is how things stand

CUBISM

My beautiful profile is glued to the ugly
profile   my young years glow
through the gravitational pull
the hope for the great love crawls
in the hardened skin
the I that I was only a moment before laughs years ago
soaring from treetop to treetop hanging from my tail like an
    ape
joined back-to-back to this other I
supple back stiff back my back   not
mine   which one is my back   her back   which
I is this   which I is that   and all
crowd simultaneously
angles paradoxes sharp colors
to cover up
the mush
of confusion

SCANNER

The scanner was moving
mapping my white bones
up and down my body
like a skilled   boring lover
Then   the dried-up technician
clicked away on a shabby computer
my body-thought
and made calculations   comparisons
and someone will decipher
what is hidden within me
and put it into a
vulgar formula
then rush away
to tell on me
to other scanning computers—
all of them horny machines
with a special kick
for human bodies

And now,
this pen is moving
across this sheet on this table.
I am dealing with this
papery aspect of my body.
And I   through the magical
palimpsest of time
see you and me sitting
now-then-now,
sending at each other breezes
transmuting into
the mute dance
of seventy-seven veils

floating with the breezy movement
of cosmic ether

Scanner Scanner tell me:
Am I starting to develop the symptoms
of Love Sickness?

Scanner Scanner look at me and tell me:
Whose bones does he think are prettier
than mine?

(tr. by the poet)

THE LOVE OF TREES

I who lack
an ancient calm
find myself hungry at their side
like a child who lacks calcium and suddenly begins
to gnaw plaster off the walls

I open my arms and embrace them
hold my body tight-tight
to their peaceful   thick trunks
from forehead
to toe
to take them in   to assimilate
their secret

And then
their simple roughness
speaks to my skin in whispering tongues
and their mute song
plays green waves in me
dissolves hard stones
of pain
softly cradles in me
wild brain waves

And I send waves
from me
onto
their rustle
onto the stillness of the earth
that nourishes them

And bit by bit
I

am no
longer I
and gradually
I am more and more
I

In more and more cells I'm able to contain
the pulse of the old trees
the pulse
of all the plants in the garden

And now
as I sit in my room
on a jittery chair
I'm drawn again to run to them

Listen   listen people:
There's nothing like a quiet embrace with a large tree
to chase away
the demons

Wings

She must   she must have angel wings
what for   why does she need angel wings?

Spread out on her stomach
it's difficult for her to fall asleep with them
they're uncomfortable
why does she need angel wings?
She's heavy
there are wings in her
there's weariness in her
there's no rest in her

> The bird is as heavy as lead
> the place she flies to
> is as black as soil
> and the bird's wing is weary
> the bird's wing is weary
> skies are thought only

The woman sheds her wings
but even without them she can't cope
only angel wings can bring relief
her wings are waves of buoyancy
her body is a sob
her wings are a bride's pure lace
with wings without wings
she has no love

> To push a wing   she thinks
> to push a wing   a bird
> through air as hard as lead
> through air as blue as a dream

Her wings are a sound
her bones a gravitational force
her body occludes light
winged and spread out on her stomach
she's a whimper yearning for calm
with wings without wings
she has no reprieve

                    The bird spreads her wings
                    half of her already flying in blue
                    the whole of her transparent in

    light

And she is as black as lead
the place she flies to
is as black as soil

                    Blue   blue
                    the bird pushes a white wing
                    skyward   skyward   skyward
                    toward the dark place
                    she aims for
                    skies   skies   skies
                    and the bird's wing is weary
                    the bird's wing is weary

Skies are thought only

GERMAN BOOT

Jerusalem, the holy city, is cold in winter,/ including holidays
and the Sabbath./
And one Friday, in early afternoon/ the clouds weren't/ red,
not even
golden, and the rain didn't/ drip like a discreet tear/ but
roughly probed
my body all over/ on Ben Yehudah Street, in the holy city of
Jerusalem./ My blond
hair turned black in the rain/ and the rain came down on me
like a blow under the belt/
and my feet hurt from the cold/ like from a terrible heartache.

Now the question is asked/ How does it happen/ that a nice
Jewish girl from a good home
parades in winter/ in the cradle of religion practically
barefoot,/ especially
since put off thy shoes* is not the point here, not to mention/
I was always weak
in Bible studies./ My dark hair clings to my forehead with a
wet kiss/ and the rain plays
havoc with my body,/ and the answer is simple and very
anti-lyrical:/
my shoe size is forty-one.

I was in Paris last summer and couldn't find/ boots my size./
I found a French lover/ discreet and experienced, but not
boots my
size./ I was in London and drank beer but no boots/ for my
large
feet/ and also in Italy, which is a professional boot,/ no boots
for me./

---

* Alludes to Exodus 3:5.

It's been seven years that I've been looking for boots,/ and
      even in heaven I thought
for sure I wouldn't find any./ And so, today, in Jerusalem, as
      the rain/ raids my body,
and my large summer shoes/ are like small Solomon pools/ in
      which
I walk/ and drown/ as the hail wrecks my body,/
on Ben Yehudah Street,/ in the window, I see boots,/ like shoes
with a long neck,/ brown, soft—and kind-eyed like Leah.

Seven years I've been laboring for Rachel barefoot with no
      shoes/ hoping for Leah
whose gaze is soft and brown on my feet/ already mad from
      pain/ from servitude/ to their size
that knows no bounds./ Seven years already that I go crazy/
      for a cover for the flesh
of my naked feet/ such turpitude in a rough Jerusalem winter/
seven years already and no boots/ in all of Jerusalem and the
      heavens too/
and here/ in the window/ sits a pair of boots/ like two lovebirds.

Oh, my soul departs and I enter/ the store behind the boots./
Oh, oh, yes, the man brings out/ of a frightful box a pair
of brown boots, or/ maroon, what's the difference, as long as
      they hug my feet/
without stifling,/ as long as they don't hang at the tip/ of my
      toes like a proverb,/
oh, hee, they mount/ mount my feet, and their brown skin/
      climbing, climbing/
up my legs, softly snuggling my ankles/ kissing my knees/ and
      stopping there.

Ay, ay, ay, what boots!/ Such leggings were never seen in all of
      Jerusalem!/
I face the mirror/ and they watch me from there,/

pretty like a pair of brown-eyed gazelles, my long legs held in
them/
and they rise even further up./ What great/ legs, what a
delightful warmth, how/
brown and warm and lovely are these boots./
Ninety pounds, says the master of the boots, and I say/ No,
seventy,
I'm just a student not even twenty. . . . /
Not possible impossible at all, absolutely not/ for it is imported/
and impossible absolutely out of the question/ for this is
extraordinary boot,/
made in/ Germany/ —
Like a blow in the feet/ and I ask: —Are you sure? Maybe
made in Sweden?/
No, absolutely not, he says, impossible/ to mistake, it says here,
"Salamander. Germany" and this/ is the most best possible./
But what about
Made-in-Israel?!/ I pull off and wildly toss the brown boots/
and what
about Made-in-Israel?!/ How come they don't have my size,/
I, who was made in Israel!/
It is only the Germans who like comfort, he replies/ in a clear
German accent,/
that's why they do so big boots/ for ladies./
—So you have nothing else?! I shout./ —Nothing.

I stood there two hours, afraid to go out into the water/ that
no doubt will rape me now,
a savage army,/ and will soil my feet./
I stood there two hours/ looking/ intermittently at skies and
boots

—And what about Volkswagen? he says to me. One/ all
right—the other no?
You can't live like that, life is/ life./ I stand in the shoe

store, my feet naked/ and cold, desperately craving the touch
    of/ Salamander./
And now my naked feet in the mirror/ seem to me/ size fifty!/
    Whereas
before, when they were wrapped/ in this overflowing beauty,
    they seemed/ size thirty./
—With Volkswagen it's different, but these are boots/ I say to
    him, my heart revolting at me./

At any rate, about two hours went by,/
—Quick lady, I close the store, tomorrow is the Sabbath,/ so
    if not now—
no boots!/ —Maybe I'll think it over tonight and if I decide
    that boots . . . .

At any rate, I stood there thinking/ about this brown skin.
    And what is
Salamander, if not a creature of fire and a creature of water
    too,/ and what about the lampshades,
and the fine skin/ of all sorts of uncles who weren't my
    uncles./ I am, indeed, an amphibian
creature/ with a practical and flexible conscience, with no/
    hangups, I'm always
in touch,/ my name is Rita, I'm totally/ uncomplicated even if
    sometimes
I read books./ What's important is comfort/ but/ Salamander
    is a water creature, industrious
and intelligent (see/ Čapek's book on the subject), that erects/
    walls under
water, erects cities/ and large dark machinery underwater,/
it's dark there, and who knows what type/ of skin it is, this
    skin may be/
suede of eyes, Leah's eyes, Sarah's, Rivkah's,/
the eyes of Rachel in face of the knife./

And these brown boots of a marvelous cut diaper my feet like
      a lover's
hand/ sculpt my ankles so that my feet/ seem almost Japanese
      in this German boot,/ and tomorrow is the Sabbath, and this
      is a God-fearing Jew, and if not today/
then when/ boots,/ and if not Salamander who is for me, oy
      to me and woe
to me, to the eyes that see this,/ my beautiful feet that look
      like this/
and the rain outside, in the Jerusalem street, a rowdy rapist/
      brutal,/ and Salamander
is a creature of fire/ burning in the fire but not consumed/ but
      the eyes of Leah,
the eyes of Sarah, the eyes of Rivkah/ the eyes of Rachel, the
      eyes of all my uncles and aunts there/
were consumed were consumed/ and here is Salamander
      burning in flames but remaining/
intact here before me/ here at my feet/
a warm blooming flame

And on a Friday afternoon/ on Ben Yehudah Street in the
      water,/
my feet in boots, and my heart in my feet,/ and the men of
      Jerusalem, Jews
and Gentiles, whistle to me/ for the legs. What a sexy pair of
      legs, says/
one Mustafa, and right after also Dani from Ramataiim,/ and
      my legs rejoice
and the warm brown skin/ so shaming/ clings to me as if it
      were my own skin/
as if I grew legs in velvety suede/ sad as the eyes
of Leah my ancient mother/ and I walk and walk through the
      streets of Jerusalem
across Katamon and Rehavia and Abu Tor and Me'ah Shearim

And my feet are warm, perhaps too warm/ this suede, and a
    wet sensation
in my feet/ perhaps after all these bastard boots do allow in a
    little/
rain, or perhaps my feet sweat as in the mikveh/* and what's
    this pressure, some blood
perhaps in the big toe/ drips through the toenail, something
    squeezed/ unknown and clammy
sticks in my feet,/ some dirt perhaps, or perhaps/
the skin rubs my skin,/ or perhaps it's just the blood/ roaring
in an orgy of warmth/ joy in the blood vessels, warm at last/
after seven cold years/ but no, it's the heel so suddenly
    clenched,/
as if caught in a thicket, held in the fist/ of Esau, Israel's
    calamity, what does it matter
if/ it was Jacob, it's the heel that hurts/ so badly, something is
    the matter
with my boots,/ but I'm already walking in Mamila Street,
    and my feet/
so sexy, a whistle here/ a squeeze there, and the blood
    erupting/
from its vessels/ from so much lust/ brownish warmish
    sweetish
and my feet take me to/ my current lover/ and he whispers:
    What
legs! and he peels off/ my flesh the sweater and/ the pants
but not yet the boots,/ and I march to the bed and the soles
thump,/ and the boots/ the boots the boots fondle my feet/
    and I'm already
spread-winged/ and my lover—on top, in heaven—wants,
    wants very much/
to shed the boots/ off my feet/ but/ the boots/ aren't shed/

---

* Ritual bath.

the boots won't be shed and won't budge/ and my lover lacks
    manners
and I lack speech/ and he tries and tries/ and they persist, the
    leeches/
and I mutter and kick/ I curse and pound my feet/
yet the boots are welded to my flesh/ and then/ he pulls out a
    knife/ tries to peel them off/
but the boots adhere/ then he pulls out a saw from under the
    pillow/ and tries to saw them off/
but they adhere adhere/ so he pulls out an axe from under the
    bed/ and tries to cleave
them/ but the boots cling/ won't let go of my feet/ so he
    swears
and pounds/ and I curse and kick/ but the boots cling/
what a dybbuk of boots!/
And my love/ in a demonic dybbuk/ begins to rip them/ a
    dybbuk fighting a dybbuk/
but suddenly pain/ all at once/ and he tears my skin/ off me/
and my love/ tears the boots off me/ and the skin/
and the boots are kicked to the floor/
and I'm a love-blazing flower
and the spot
I lie on
holy
and my spirit fades in smoke
and the entire world swoons
and the secular angels in heaven
call out Holy Holy
and my feet
red
with shame

INTERNAL GYMNASTICS

In order to rend
you must exercise morning and evening morning and evening
you must exercise many many
years
the frail   will-muscle
(one-two   one-two)

In order to mend
you must exercise morning and evening   morning and evening
the feeble   memory-muscle
(three-four   three-four)

In order to swim in the mud
you must exercise again and again   again and again
the tiny   rage-muscle

In order not to drown in the air
you must exercise more and more and more and more
the slacking   slacking muscle
of your right to exist

In order to flee
you must breathe deeply   and—
feel the muscle of letting go of pain
the muscle of letting go of pain
(one-two-three-four)

And now   yes   a good massage on
the letting-go-of-hurt muscle
(does it hurt?)
and massage more and more
the muscle of unforgiveness
(ugh   what a knotty muscle!)

And now
in order not to flee
you must try to feel
the muscle of self-love
(where is it   where is it   where is it?
where is it   where is it   where is it?!)

(the voice of the teacher grows faint)

one-one-one-one
one-one-one-one

(the voice of the teacher fades)

Hey-hop!   Hey-hop!
Hey-hop!   Hey-hop!
Hey-hop!   Hey-hop!
Hey-hop!   Hey-hop!

Hey . . . .

(the voice is no more
as if it never was)

SUB-MATTER

I sail   sail   sail
in the vast space of the sub-matter
of my minutely minuscule life

Between a flickering particle of will
and a flashing particle of will
a galactic space
of no will   is sprawled on its back
snoring
at times stirring a muscle   (a foot
a finger   a nostril)   while dreaming
a sweet   deceitful
dream of fierce desires   of great life
movements

And somewhere   among
particles of will   between a proton of longing
and a photon of aversion—
light years
of dim twilights
of nothing

Three Women, Strangers, Watch Me by the Sea

I sit by the sea
watch it with craving eyes
cuddle with its soft quilts
grow hydroponic plants from seeds
of small fancies   tossed
against the water
between horizons
and depths

And three women, strangers, at the next table
drive hard eyes into
my darkness
invade the chambers of my body
raid my small bit of privacy
so blue and chlorophyllic

And I become a yellowish rustle
and rage drills black stripes through me

And the sea   the sea is indifferent
launching toward me   and toward them   its insatiable
    waves
in a kind of great neutrality
observing me   and them   with the same blue   craving eyes

The sea
the great lover
carries on

From *A Hidden Passenger* (1999)

ORGANISM, CHAOS

The sea   the rocks   the seagulls—
for a moment I felt how we're all
one organism
the sea   the woman eating kebab at the table across
and I
or what I try in vain to hold onto for a moment
as a self
inside the riptide of the internal sea
and the large cup of coffee   hot   courting my soul
like a small devil

And especially the sea   the sea

And so   for a moment I felt
but instantly
forgot
what I'm
feeling
and the hard woman leaning with carnal
devotion over her plate

The seagulls   that only a moment before sat on the rocks
spread in the sky like a fan
and by the time I'd written "seagulls"
were already settled on another rock
and the sea   the sea is distant   apart
a great beast   independent
a gigantic organism

The gorging woman raises her hand
and places it on her belly   aahhhh
and I   and I   so very much do not
want to be one organism with her

And what about this sparkling piece of sky
that right this minute a few clouds detach from it
and what about?

These lines
fragmented even more than these bits of clouds
they too are chaos

So what? What?
Am I leaning over the fleeting moment-plate
with carnal devotion?

Over there   across   beyond the glass   a wonderful fatherly-
        motherly church
the color of mustard   with a turquoise grid

And from the other side
the sea calls me

And I where am I

LET ME HAVE A BOWL

I don't have the power to try
to catch
flowing entities
I don't have the power to capture
visible and invisible halos
I don't have the power to touch
unfathomable air
oracular lights
or the gilded edges
of souls

Let me have a simple existence
following Newton's laws of physics
let me sit in a chair
lie on a bed
walk on a sidewalk
let me place a hand on
a solid wood table
rather than on a void dotted here and there
with crumbs of shadows
of particles of inscrutable energy

Let someone
place a benevolent hand on me
let me have a beautiful warm dress
let me have a bowl of onion
soup

Greenhouse Effect

Today is the warmest day ever
recorded in the past one hundred years
worldwide.
This confirms the theory of the greenhouse effect.
This confirms that we have no claim to special felicity
on this planet   that giant icebergs will melt collapse and
        flood
this tiny   blue   planet
circling like a small innocent screwball

No basis for felicity

This thought cuts through me like a speedy neutron as I
cross the street toward the kiosk to buy
cigarettes and chocolate   a bit of drugging
for the soul   supine   soiled
upon the lowly floor of my existence.
So here goes. The greenhouse effect.
Chaim tells me he has read that he who is smart
should buy a house in a cold zone.   Where?   Siberia?
        Radioactive pollution.
Norway?   Darkness and suicide.   And near me
in our tiny steamy country
loved ones
so dear to me   bravely uphold
their frail lives
so frail

If only someone's prayer
a torn prayer   tongue-tied
if only it had

the power
of the butterfly effect*
to subvert
subvert
subvert
the law
of the greenhouse effect

To alleviate the edict
of the horror effect

What
what did I say?

---

* Term given to the phenomenon formulated in Edward Lorenz's question: "Does the flap of a butterfly's wings in Brazil set off a tornado in Texas?" (James Gleick, *Chaos: Making a New Science* (New York: Viking Press, 1987) (Author's note.)

The Glow of the Child

The glow of the child grows dim
greedily life consumes his light
his kinship with the clean wind grows weak
already the rays of the sun touch him less frequently
he grows imprisoned in words

The child grows harder in a human shield
that hardens like scar tissue
around what is soft and wondrous and human

The child grows to resemble those who are no longer
children. He himself when he goes past a soft glowing
      child
he looks at him
as one discovering a lost
continent

And I   as I grieve over this and put these words to paper
no longer notice when the soft pain   babyish
breaks in me through
the scar tissue that is
me

And this carves in me an added pain   and all of me
is alight with electricity
and is soon
charred

Pictures from a Diary

suckling

My child
five hundred seventy nine days and nights
you sucked my milk   for you I turned myself into a warm
    whitish ball
I gathered myself around me-you every hour   daynight
    daynight
you sucked and sucked   my body gave up the hunger for
  , sleep   I
    became for you
a soothing fountain   I gave gave   I gave-received   I
    gave-received
I was all love
I was a vessel of love

weaning

Now   to deny   to hide   to become estranged
to hear you wail with longing   and not relent
I want to bite myself   to hurt myself as I hurt you

not

Not to be with your child when you are with him
to feel for the first time how you close off to him
to respond to him absentmindedly   absent emotionally
    physically
not to be with him when you're with him
letting this bubbling spring   letting this being
stir around you   and you push it away calmly   you withdraw
calmly   fighting for some territory of your own   dubious
fighting tooth and nail for some I-me   dubious

feeling how the ropes
of longing
thick and coarse
bruise your hands
as you pull them toward you forcibly   trying to overcome
their power

to drown

The child slips in the bath tub   nearly fractures his small
    skull
the fragile walls of existence fall on you.   Mad with worry
you try to explain to your child that you are, in fact, a tomato
someone is trying to squash—a moment before it blows up.
He laughs   and again slips from your hands,   nearly drowns
    in the water.
A roar rises from your gut.
Like stamping the paw of a dragon in soft   golden clay
so it is   when you blast your nerves
into the white-milk essence of your child.
And he opens astonished eyes at you
and your noises engulf him   smoke and fire threaten
to infiltrate the caves of his breathing.
And only the deep-rooted love   solid   fills him with a balm
impervious to your noises and looks you
straight in the eye

is it from me

"Bone of her self,   flesh of her flesh."*
Your separateness.

---

* A play on: "And Adam said, This is now bone of my bones, and flesh of my flesh:
she shall be called Woman, because she was taken out of Man." (Genesis 2:23).

The astonishment: Is it from me that this wondrous creature
    came?
From my flesh—this luminosity?   From inside me—this
    force?
Force.   Fragile, fragile.   To soothe him.
And to always shield him.

the world

The world for you is the warmth of my arms   my breasts
    my laugh.
The colored forms that adorn the bars of your crib.   Your
    rough tongue
seeking my nipple.   Light.   Window.   The copper bell that
    daddy
brought you.
Shimshon playing the flute.   Miriam singing to you.*
Seemingly,   a small world.
But you know   (and I too fleetingly sense)
that this is the greatest of all worlds

---

* Shimshon and Miriam are the child's grandparents.

SPACE POCKETS

Space pockets   time pockets
things that enclose
things that are no more—
tempt me
to pickpocket
myself

Rubber nets as safety nets
to jump on them like trampolines
to fall in them in fatal
falls
from the heights of this circuitous circus

In the pockets of my warped time—
the tearing to pieces of the living flesh
of loved ones
as I attempt restrained coexistence with terrific background
        music
to which nonetheless the body is indifferent
a heaviness that squeezes the contents of the belly
blends with crumbs of a terrific snack
the daily inventory is woven into braids with terrific
science fiction notions of some Robert Sheckley
that someone insists on telling me about right now

What do I care about Sheckley!
In my world—
an exacting reality
steely causalities
iron laws
gravity sweeping giant planets
onto orbits of no deviation

iron laws
of no imagination at all

And I
like a frightened ant
don't know
where
to run
where
to be crushed
where
to put
the pain I feel for him
for him   for us   for me
how to bring him joy
I who
have forgotten
the flesh of joy
oy
let me have a small pocket
to cuddle in
and forget
everything

Laundry

The washing machine that churns inside me
takes a brief break
the unnerving rumble   stops
it lays its hooves under its belly
the gurgle of the kill   calmed
I pull out of its maw   one by one
each item
after the boiling
after the spinning
one   by   one
I spread them   hang them
on a clothesline
swinging in the wind

Here is the fear of death
I've learned to be its subservient subtenant
but I haven't learned to look it
in the eye

Here it is
fastened to the line with plastic clothespins
dyed optimistic yellows and greens
it flutters slightly in the warm breeze
slowly
drying

Here is the beloved man
a delicate flower
a slender stem
withering

His figure emerges toward the backdrop of laundered linens
attempts to become
one of them

Fluttering
held tight with red and black
clips

His likely life
and the unlikely
they too flutter
striking each other
among fabrics that have been beaten down by pounding
that have risen
from the bottom of the bottom
from the boiling heat of the abyss

and made their way to the roof
to break a brutal noon light

to whiten

The Objects

The objects are done for the day.
The cup of water empty.
The telephone mute.   The handbag sits on the armchair
after a hectic day of errands with its stomach full.
It vomited all.
My son's rocking horse hasn't rocked
in years. Now   late night   it's a pony
forever sculpted.
The piano, too, is shut   abandoned.   Its gleaming teeth
hidden behind
a mute   tight mouth.
The television   the eye of a Cyclops
large   cold   and   spellbinding
now shut. Guiltless.

Everyone around me is asleep.   The room is quiet.
It allows me into its bosom with forbearing indifference.
Now   at night   when my myriad threads are loose
and my myriad springs lax   now at night
when I'm done being such a useful person
to so many objects   people   errands
I, too, become   a thing
of no menace.
An abandoned object   placid   blameless.

Inert.

NEARLY

On my sky-blue flannel sheet
white sheep   sheep and tiny stars
to count in my sleep.
Beyond the reading lamp on my right, the breathing of my
        child
and the hum of the humidifier.
On my left,   the small blue radio humming scraps of songs.
Beyond the wall   neighbors sleep.
Beyond the house   other houses.
Let there be another billion people
cuddling at this moment
one into the other
breathing
on sky-blue sheets.
Outside   a great chill   and beyond our Mediterranean city
snow is falling.
Beyond the layers of dark clouds   stars shine.
Nearly bliss.

SUCKLING

The universe suckles the milky way
the milky way suckles the solar system
the solar system suckles the earth
the earth suckles us
into it

We suckle the earth
the earth suckles the solar system
the solar system suckles
the milky way that suckles the cluster of galaxies
that suckles the universe

And all of us
loll and bawl in the bosom
of God

From *Portrait of Father and Daughter* (2004)

To Watch Life

To watch life
from inside a hospital
(a large large house
of many-many)—

Like watching
a beautiful butterfly
from the underside of its
black belly

I PUT OVER MY HEAD

I put over my head
the large white envelope
containing the C.T. images
of my father
in a day fraught with anxiety
in a week fraught with anxiety
in months fraught with anxiety
in years fraught with anxiety
in a scorching high noon
I violated the C.T. images
of my father
to protect my foolish face
from idiotic
sun spots

I'M SITTING

I'm sitting biting my nails
in the corridor of the health clinic
in the corridor painted red-white
I sit and bite the cuticles
of my pitiful fingernails
as I'm thinking
what will be the result and what
will the doctor say and what
will the instrument tell
and what will the numbers say
and what will the lab stir up and what
will the computer spit out
about his body
his innocent body

AND HOW YOU'RE TRYING TO MAKE ME LAUGH

a conversation

Daddy, I'm going down to the store. Can I get you
    something?
Yes.
What?
A piano.
How many?
Three and half kilos.
What color?
Rouge.

This Man

This man lying in bed
and you're trying to infuse his body
with healing powers
you've sucked from the essence of your bodysoul
and you're trying to infuse him with health
and you're trying to make him better
to rouse his collapsing internal organs

This man
for a moment
seems eternal to you
for a moment
a mortal here   here   it's happening
right before your gaping eyes
right before your eyes veiled in prayer
right before your eyes veiled in fear
here   here   he rises   luminous
radiating life   hued gold and green
here   here   he's convulsed in a twisted reddish-brown
here   he's a still body
bearing the mistakes of careless doctors
here   he's a packed sack that worn-out nurses hasten to turn
    over
and be done with the shift
this man   here   he's all spirit
here   he's all pricked with tubes
here   he's the whole of the small universe granted him
by God
here   he is getting better
here   he is getting poisoned by the hospital's infections
here   he climbs the torn rope-ladder
of your wild hope
here   he drops to the floor
of this wretched circus called

Life
here here you're saving him
here here they're saving him
here here you abandon him
this victim of blunders
to the jaws of this preying beast
squatting between the white walls the white smocks
and the prevalent ghastliness
masquerading in white
here he is yours
here he is of
the ravenous void
here he is fully absorbing your
marrow as you're trying to trickle it into him
in a touch lighter than air
here you infuse the whole of you into him
here he is no more
withdrawing from your life
leaving you
to a sobbing sigh
to a sigh of relief selfish selfish
a sigh
that your hunger for sleep   for rest
tears in the flesh of his life

Here is this man so dear to you
lying motionless   prancing before you in a frenzy
the whole of him made of shifting
mosaic fragments of hope and despair and a round soft-
    fleshed prayer
and a sharp-toothed doubt tearing
tearing chunks in you

Here is this man

And he's your father

*

When I came in here today
a woman asked me
how I was and where I had been

I asked her do you remember him
and she said sure
and I didn't know what's behind her sure

But the whole of you
emerged before my thousand eyes
filling up
the hollow of my body

Father Who Comes and Appears

Father   who comes and appears in my life in every possible
form
as memory clouds
as the innocent object of prayers
as items no one wants anymore
and last night   as a man absolutely alive in a dream
who has risen to life and leads another life
in another neighborhood

Daddy who comes
and goes
where are you
where are you
really

From *Secret Details from the Transparent Binder*
(2007)

THE CUTE WORD-STROLLERS

The words fled from me—

Baby-strollers
cushioned with pink and blue lace
with nonabsorbent oilcloth
with soft sheets to love
the bruised skin

And so
they fled
from under my hands
that rock with compulsive love
the unruly cradle
of life

From under my hand
rocking with a desperate motherly passion
the tiny cradles of life
that I've been trying to spread under the underside
of every thing in this life

They fled from me
all the pink baby-strollers
all these cute words on wheels

They fled from me
they fled from me
down this steep incline

More and More They Wrap

More and more they wrap around me
the shrouds of incomprehension
more and more they pad
my feelers
more and more they weave inside me
a soft rug
that fully absorbs my footsteps
and I no longer hear my footsteps
as I try to get to the bottom
of things
more and more I stumble into walls—
indulgent   walls
so familiar
with the blind-dumb of my kind
who strike them with feeble hands
who attempt to walk upon them
and, falling short,
they rub their heads against the walls
to relieve their sorrow
like cats   that know   with feline sorrow

that they will never reach the bottom of things

nor the surface

WHEN PAIN BECOMES A FLOWER

When pain becomes a flower
when the odor of danger
becomes the scent
of a cultivated narcissus—

I flee

When flower becomes pain
when the roots suddenly turn
baring teeth
when the odor of a sharp   blazing danger
is released at once
from the clenched fist—

I come forward

METAPHORS

You want from me
metaphors
(that I once used)
as in:
"A gigantic bird spreads its wings the size of continents."

And I say:
The resplendent bird   soaring
doesn't capture my heart

My heart is captured
in the thicket of the tiny commotion
of particle-waves
in the transparent black
in the multicolored rainbow
of the gray

You want from me
fireworks

And I   I want
only to expunge
from my lips with my tongue
the bitter-salty taste
of gunpowder

HERE IN THE HIDDEN HOUSE

Here   in the hidden house named after
Bialik's wife   in back of the main
house   Bialik's otherworldly home

Here   under palm trees   and other trees
saved from the felling axe   from destruction
near a small pool of illusions
they resurrect Menashe Levin*
a little known genius
who died long ago

And in front of me—
the shaded back of his wife Masha

On the stage—
throbbing flashes and flickers of darkness
of stroboscopic recall
intermittently   boogie   intermittently
freeze in the dark
in the wacky lighting of the oblivion disco

And a scholar
who is a star-geologist of deep heavens
launches fragments of phrases
flashing   soaring

Behind
the speakers   the words   the boogie of the lame memory
a white wall   white
throbbing   blank
inviting to be etched in black

_____

* Hebrew author.

And I   clad in violet embroidered slacks—
violet* against desertion
against oblivion ---

And a few streets away—
beyond the proud   oriental domes of palm trees
and small lemon trees enduring on their own—
they dream
dream forever
the dead
of the cemetery
named after the one-armed
hero**
and among them   also dreaming forever is the poet
and also his wife
who long ago ---
in this house ---

And over there   almost here
no one tries anymore
they're all laid out in their dreams
in a darkness
that has no   has no beats
a darkness that no memory flashes
could overcome

---

* Also means remedy, balm.
** Joseph Trumpeldor (1880–1920), a Zionist activist who lost an arm in battle.

ANTS

Tiny ants in an anthill
toil rush work work
cute ants in ant-tunnels dig build sweat shift
delicate ants in ant-city birthing raising feeling braving
nothing ants in ant-world think toil try meditate
tiny ants cute ants labor labor hurry diligent
work work cultivate nurture build haul perceive blind
rush run want want a million ants in a tiny
anthill
in a tiny yard   they believe   a great and infinite kingdom
comma ants in ant-universe plan future present future
delicate ants in ant-hole mash love feel responsible
quick-quick gray red brown white black ants
sweet ants carry on marching bearing crumbs of thought
strong ants tiny ants nothing ants
work work rush forever   their lives go by in tunnels of hope
with great   very great effort
they don't know   have no concept   no trace of a concept
have no suspicion   no hint of a suspicion
that a boorish foot
large and boorish
is approaching the nest
approaching in a second
to smash   to squash   cute ants nothing ants
and now   nothing
a hole

In Such a Furnace of Noon

In such a furnace of noon
as the scorching light strips
the skin from the flesh
as the pavements boil and the terror of existence
simmers
as wars bare their teeth
as people rise in the morning and die in the evening
in such a furnace of noon
I find myself a refugee
of the burning furnace
in a cool corner
and next to me   other refugees like me who fled
to the periphery of the inferno
a cream-pie a milkshake a cigarette some flirting
the drug of the newspaper and other addictions inside which
we huddle   fearful
inside sterilized bubbles surrounded by a raging plague

Everything
everything is just
huddling corners above the abyss
and there we cuddle
in our mouth the flavorful taste of the strawberry
we bite into,   like in that Buddha fable,
hanging with one hand onto a parched vine
that will soon be uprooted
while above us
a tiger waits
and beneath us
at the bottom of the abyss
another tiger
waits

We hold tight
at the precipice
fill our mouth with a red strawberry   oozing
as we muse:
"What a marvelous strawberry!"

So Why Don't I

So
why don't I take my bundles
pack everything and flee to Arad—
when mustard bombs are about to explode
and nerve gas bombs
and deadly virus bombs?
Because
first the need to exchange the Jell-O at the grocer's
and first the need to hang the wash
and first the need to go to judo class   the kid
so he'd be strong
and besides
because
life
is a thing
that hypnotizes
because
first the need to get over the cold
and first the need to sign up for the pool
and pay the phone bill before they disconnect
and all this
because
life is a thing that hypnotizes
and first I need to finish my sandwich

DON'T TELL ME

Don't tell me
that now there's a perspective
to history

Today there's no perspective
to what has happened before
no more
than tomorrow there will be
a perspective to what
happens today

Everywhere   everywhere
blindness masquerading
as wisdom

A desperate void masquerading
as something else

Even the snake of time—history
the one that clutches its tail in its mouth
doesn't know
guesses
imagines that it's holding something
worthy of note   imagines   imagines

Don't tell me

Double Exposure in the Black Forest

The month of May in a beautiful city named Freiburg
set between green hills a lush meadow and amazing mountains
the month of May in a beautiful city named Freiburg, sitting
    calmly
like a saint bathed in light and grace.
The cobblestones under footsteps of hundreds of years
spring water flowing in small canals along the sidewalks
in a beautiful city named Freiburg toy houses simulate ancient
    castles
shops look like candy fancy restaurants serve exquisite
    asparagus
a beautiful city, this Freiburg in Germany,
and I sit under a glowing chandelier   sucking on an
    asparagus sprig
but something goes awry and behind every golden Aryan child
there appears another child
his skull smashed
and at every table of carved wood   sits a laughing group of
    S.S. officers
and in the sweet shops of Freiburg I try on pink shirts and
    green shoes
and in every shop window I see piles of frayed shoes
    orphaned
the shoes of old people
the shoes of children
and in every hair salon piles of wonderful hair shaved from
    scalps
and under every glowing chandelier I see captains
poring over exact plans for exact crematoria
and in the (wonderful) department store in Freiburg
I buy a game for my son   Shoot the Target
and in the green meadow   from an electric power pole   a
    Jew hangs

and over the shoulder of every red-cheeked youth   a human
   skeleton peers
and beyond each pair of eyes in the street   a pair of Jewish
   eyes   dimmed
and near a wooden shack in a sweet forest
the moans of Jews hiding for years in a hole
and the sound of approaching engines   approaching
blends in with the tunes of swanky music in the album
a man gave me, he who called me Sweetie in German,
   plotting to have me,
and I saw black and gave him a cold shoulder
and in my adorable room at The Black Forest Hotel I stroke
   with my fingers
the wooden rustic dresser and immerse myself in a soothing
   bubble bath in Freiburg
and now, May 1989, in this saintly beatific Freiburg
upon the round pavement stones   millions of steps like a
   flood
of processions going to their death
a death you can speak only in German
and this dark fertile soil
heaves and rises and above it sway from side to side
bodies in white
dead-alive-dead
pressed together
their flesh transparent
in dusklike light   lamenting without a sound
and the mountains and lush valleys rise and the soil is gripped
   in labor contractions
and I in a soft bed in The Black Forest Hotel am tossed inside
a nutshell among the breakers
holding onto the frame of my bed holding onto transparent
   bodies
so as not to drop
from the world

A Half-Day Off

Forcibly I tore myself
from the network of ropes in which I'm always entangled
carved for myself a slice of a half-day
break   to take a train ride to Haifa with my child

The world prepares its bosom for us
my son's all set for takeoff

A half-day off
a half-day off—
what a midsummer night's dream!
What a living beauty!
And I sit in the train   and suddenly discover
that I carry excess baggage:
large brown suitcases of refugees   tattered
inside them winding tunnels
along which my soul always creeps
lugging within all sorts of reckoning
a cacophony of head-stomach prattle that stands between me
and open fields
and sucks
the juice of my mini-tour

And these   and others   travel with us
on the train to Haifa
for a half-day off
that I took for myself by force
from everything
and they bite
into my half slice of pink pie
which I've tried to snatch
my half sweet-measly slice

And I try to push these suitcases
aside
and the sea too tries
to seep through me
but the suitcases sit tight in my stomach
and the sea nudges them a little
and the skies try too
they too try

And maybe
just maybe
I'll have a few seconds
of freedom
today with my child
on this optimistic train
to Haifa

Love at McDonald's

I love my child at McDonald's
love him terribly
released from asinine kitchen duties
from the taxing commitment to healthy nutrition

He devours a Double Mac of oozing meat
I chain-smoke French-fried cigs
he gulps a gallon of Coke   I down my third cup of coffee

Suddenly I have time to look
straight into his eyes
suddenly I have time to write down
this small confession

How this collective sin
liberates!
How this cosmopolitan conglomerate
contributes to calm the family unit!

In the large glass panes are reflected
tiny cold neon lights
and beyond them the city flickers
its amity

And everything
everything at this moment seems
to be an ally

THE CAT FRASIER AS A PHILOSOPHY MAJOR

Daddi loves the cat Frasier
Daddi also loves Tsili and Gili   they're also cats   I love them
    too
but Frasier in particular

The cat Frasier   red-haired   pensive
observes   for hours   deep in thought
a dripping pipe
drip   drip
probes   a slick wall
lick   lick
an entire night   tries to find
meaning
and I observe Daddi who observes Frasier   who observes
a different wall every night   a different pipe
in other words   she reads this philosopher and another

Daddi is rapt   studying her   delighted
he strokes   she purrs   stiffens   then contemplates

Daddi contemplates her   I contemplate her   him   and the
    air trembles

She sits   present with a pure presence
then rises from her studies   stretches in a yoga tiger stretch
rises   rubs a quivering coiled tail against Daddi's ankle   my
    ankle
then lets go   sits down to a short meditation—
the cat of Pure Reason

Daddi gazes at her   a pure gaze   a quivering body
and I   I am nothing compared to her   to him

A Moment Tries to Catch Itself by Its Tail

The fear of life and death
fused with jazz   the noise of buses and tiny lusts
the round electric lamps
are reflected in the greenish transparent binder
like haughty bright moons

The worry for her
who is dear to me dear
digs holes in me

A woman walking by with a baby carriage
fills
my blood vessels to the brim

And from afar
a well pointed
rocket

The small waitress is made to fit the model
of a professional flirt
she resembles a cake
while from afar   from afar
a rocket glares

The small doggy frantically barks
at every macho dog that goes by

My own great organ
is silent

And from the northeast
a battery of rockets
aims to harm

Why do I clutch a pen
at this very moment
as if clutching a sword

My young son is about to enlist

And this
constricts
all my blood vessels

CINEMA

If my life is a movie—
I am a deserted movie house

An audience of one person
(also me)
watching
one eye shut
the other crossed
a torn film

And so   I sit with myself at the end of the day
sinking in a mountain of popcorn
pieces of the movie I've lived through
are screened inside me
forward and backward
bits of images   bits
of a dark void   jump-cuts to other movies
I haven't been to
crunching popcorn salt and butter
loudspeakers amplify the soundtrack that's thunderous to
    begin with
loud voices and thunder drown the image
a camera scurries a lens blurs—

And I miss most of the movie

IF ONLY I WERE A FEARLESS BIKER

If only I were a fearless biker tearing
the roads of my life refusing
to relent simmering with rage leaning over the handlebars
of the Destroyer whose explicit name we must not voice
in the network of respectable roads
let me hurl my life into danger
fastening together past present future with the cry of the
    shofar* welding together
forwardbackwardeverywhichway
breaking through fences open to every racing wind a herd of
    wild unbridled colts
adjusting to ever-present dangers no stingy speed limits for
    me
I draw myself like a blade from breakfast bread riding my mad
    mechanical horse
thundering tearing like a rogue wave through shallow water
ripping through splitting rivers of metal thundering rowing in
    slalom after
slalom spinning at the brink of the drop and hop across to the
    opposite side
defying the force of gravity daring
daring the horny fate laying myself down on the road to the
    right
laying myself down to the left triumphant my body draws in
    demonic shivers
spirals of eights and more eights kissing infinity
tearing my virginity anew morning morning moment
    moment hurtinglovinghurting
loving forever

* A ram's horn. Mentioned in the Bible and the Talmud, the shofar was used in an-
cient times to announce holidays, and is blown in synagogues on Rosh Hashana and
at the conclusion of Yom Kippur.

147

and I am hanging by a thread   if only
I had sped up my life to crash the security
walls of the law engraved like a taboo in stone
my daredevil self breezing typhoons
blowing last year's smoke like a dragon blowing
from the carburetor
of my spent
life

And on second thought:

If only I had a tricycle bike
and on its side   just in case   a rescue
craft

And please let me not
God-forbid
harm
even an ant

Sixty-Five Million Years Ago

Sixty-five million years
ago
seven tenths
of all life forms
were eradicated
off the face
of the earth

Nights
I become very small
the dark renders me
in the right dimensions

I turn into
a tiny islet
hungry for sleep
and wishing
only
that the great waters
do not
flood it

SHORT ONES

I still find it hard to digest
that behind every lit window
a life-story hides
no less
profound
than my own

*

The light reflected in the glass
was golden and round and perfect.
I took a pen into my hand,   to wax poetic about the moon.

In the middle of the first line I realized:
The reflection of a streetlamp.

*

What a decadent treat.
To exercise short poems
Japanese style
while hauling a mammoth
on your back

*

You ask that I tell you about my life
in the forty minutes you've allotted me.
To try and pull two fine hairs
from a heap of hippopotamuses
in a river of mud.

*

I love her because
she raises the level

of serotonin in my brain
which makes me feel good

*

From nearby tables phrases rise
scrappy   zesty.
How to tell my delighted ears
that these are only
light ripples
across an ocean
of tragedies

*

I too try my hand
writing shorts.
The hand fans enfolding a thousand folds
let them wait

*

A white cloud a small cloud.
A short span.
The scent in the wake of

And then I became

FROM THE DIARY OF A PENGUINETTE
(fragments found after the extinction of the species)

In our language there are seven words.
The first two are:
Kwu: Cold
Kwu Kwu: Colder
I was a modest, slow penguinette
in one of the poles
in an endless night

Yes   I was a penguinette
black and white
innocent and wise
standing forever
in the corner
of the world

There   in the black pole
the snow lit somewhat the existential dark

We were a community of multitudes standing
waiting for nothing

I shuffled a bit to the right a bit to the left
but had no space for choice

Each season I lay an egg

Hatching it throughout a night without end
throbbing a small Penguinnish hope

In our language there are seven words.
The next two are:

Kwee: Yes
Kwo: No

Suddenly
I twitched a bit

A million Penguins
stood   amazed
looking ahead as one
to the sea
in the black
polar
silence

We are a crowded community
perhaps because
we are surrounded
by endless
void

In our language there are seven words.
The next two are:
Oh: Black
Ah: White

I don't understand what suddenly
made me—
an anonymous Penguinette—
turn in the other direction.

I don't understand what made me turn.

And so   on an iceberg
I stood through the long night

molding dark
giving rhythm to silence

I don't understand

After a long   cruel night
in the other direction
I suddenly became aware that
the other direction   too
is the same

Because in our pole
forward is backward
and sideways to here   is like
sideways to there

I changed direction   and stuttered
with my small   webbed feet
to the other side—
that is,   to the same

I was a homely   dedicated Penguinette
with a bit of unruly   yellow tuft
sticking out insolent
of the black down on my head

Our favorite pastime is this:
we, multitudes upon multitudes
are standing together   waiting for
all

The seventh word in Penguinnish
is the richest:
Kwee-Kwo-Ah-Oh:
Food

When I used to think about
food (Kwee-Kwo-Ah-Oh)—
my loyal mate used to brood,
hatching on our
eternal egg
not remembering what
he is sitting on

When I used to bow to my partner—
he would offer me a smooth stone for a gift

My female   modest   Penguinnish life
was suddenly enriched   Kwee

Here   now   he is suddenly calling:
Kwoo --- Kwoo --- Kwo --- Oh!

We are all looking in the first
direction:
The ocean is soaring in a giant wave
the ocean is nearing   sweeping ---

But we haven't got a word
for it

(tr. by the poet)

Mrs. Darwin

Mrs. Darwin is sitting and knitting.
Her husband is absent
from home   each time   a year   or two
sailing to the Galapagos Islands
stooping over fossils.
She is sitting   waiting   knitting
theorizing:

Evolution   Evolution   Evolution.
(knitting a stitch   another stitch   another stitch)
But who created this Mechanism of
Evolution?
Who   c r e a t e d   this big   hesitant Woman—
whom he calls   Eve-olution?
Who   c r e a t e d   this woman,
who   with tiny tremors   imperceptible
to the human eye
(She is starting a new row)
moved herself   bit   bit   tremor   tremor
from one tenuous phase
(stitch)
to
(stitch)
another tenuous phase   hesitant   tentative
(stitch)
up this rope ladder   oh   so fine
(stitch)
so   maddeningly   slowly?

Who   c r e a t e d   her—
(row)
since it is   after all   apparent
that, like our Mother Eve,

(another row)
she too had to be torn apart
from the c r e a t e d rib
of c r e a t e d Adam—
(new row)
so she, too, Ms. Evolution—
in order to begin   to get started
in order to be moved
in order to begin to move—
(stitch stitch stitch stitch)
some Thing
had to
ignite
some tiny spark of hers
some tiny spark of all this.
No?
(The needles freeze.)

And out of what
was ignited the teeny-tiniest
beginning
of all this bizarre
well-planned co-
incidence—
had it not been for
(silence. And now fast-fast another row)
Creation?!

In other words   there was someone who Created!
No?

And so Mrs. Darwin is sitting in
her parlor   missing him   knitting

And he   when he is back home
from the other side of the globe
with his Theory filling his head—
she offers him the woolen sweater
which she knitted

And he?   Gives her a kiss
takes the sweater for his next trip
runs away
to the other side of the world
with his cute theory

And she?   She is sitting again alone
starting to knit the next sweater
and knows that the first stitch
is always being moved
by her love for Charlie

Thus she is thinking   Mrs. Darwin
and the stitch suddenly
drops   undone
and the whole row
is unraveled

(tr. by the poet)

From *Witches* (2009)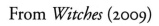

A Witch Bent on Healing

A pit has opened before me   I must
leap into it   fill it as much as I possibly can
someone's wound   a wound of a beast   a man   a universe
is spread before me
I must approach   approach   drip myself
into it   to become healing drops
to suck its contaminated blood into me
to drink the pus
to lay myself atop as white gauze

The Witch Who Did Not Cushion Her Life

One day she rose and understood that
she has no cushion
that her life is based on error
the bones bare the marrow vulnerable
she has nothing to fall back on
an error like an open wound in the junction
of her solar plexus nerves
her stomach muscles turn into a brutal iron shield
but it too will not cushion her
on cold nights, self-pity a pillow under her head
the wisdom of the wise, the weary, and the bitter
a pure sheet for her body
how pure the sheet on her body
tiny muscle spasms flutter in her   trying to flee
but she won't flee
the star nearest to her extinguished galaxy
is *Proxima Centauri*
and it explodes four light-years away!
Even the nearest star isn't near!

On cold dark nights like these
the burning fire   at least   is a certainty
the fire
a warm   anticipation

MUTANT WITCH

Meantime   she digs
removes layer after layer
dives into the depths of the history
of her body   attempts to decipher
her genetic code

She will not reach it

Meantime   an archeologist of her flesh

her head is heavy   bent   inclined
like the head of an elderly scientist

From the corner of the window will pounce
all at once a black cat   sensual
she will rise from the floor   comb her hair
the electric lamp will glow   a breeze of fresh air
will restore a lost equilibrium to the furniture   which began
already to shift in a slant   as in a sinking ship

Again she digs inside her body   to uncover its beginning
its dark mutation

Her body will not yield to her

Witch Breaks

Words that have lost the power to sprout
the music of springwater
the timidity of the virginal
the thunder of a volcano
the marvelous fragrance of a newborn—
such words break in my mouth   in my teeth
and if they don't break
I break them
to stick out my tongue at the world

to release from the pain of ruins
the essence of breath

WITCH IN FACT

You hear "witch"
and imagine a flowing black cloak
a broom sweeping the heavenly winds
flight with the motion of a tiny pinky
a resolve that can shift continents

You haven't got a clue.
The cloak is ripped in the wind and must be sewn daily.
The legs are stricken with palsy.
All day the magic broom mops up
filth.   Nights you have to wash it
and hang it to dry.
The steely resolve   has no steel.
It is cast in fatigue and hardened pulp.
True   it is strong   but is easily broken.
My decisions are a devilish dance
of yes embraced by no   yes struck by no
yes defeated by no   no defeated by yes.
The good intentions swell up,   a drape in the wind,
but the thin drape is threadbare   full of holes.
And yes,   I, too, am full of holes.
And also suffer from rheumatism

HOPEFUL WITCH

The fat   rosy   hope
chases me away
I cower at her door
I scratch
her door
she kicks me
I weep at her gate
I crawl back
to her
I rub against her
ask forgiveness
she swallows me
I swallow her

The Witches' Chorus

As we gallop on the horses of fire
the saddle scrapes our skin
down there.
And the tailbone pops in the ride
and it hurts
down there.
It is hard for us to withstand the poisonous hiss
of the whispers about us.
The men feel threatened
the women feel threatened
the community won't embrace us.
We can't make a living. We can't pay the landlady
for the pitiful room.
Yes,   a witch, too, has a body.
We, too, are flesh
and blood. Blood and flesh
and a mutation:
a dysfunctional
flight organ

MONOLOGUE OF THE WITCH IMPREGNATED BY THE DEVIL

I can hold in my belly all
the heavenly angels all the small
demons of hell.   I have enough warmth
to wrap the world in a down cover.
In it drill for me dens of love.
Let them not tell me I'll give birth to a monster.
All the bells of the depth ring madly
in the depths of my womb.   When a man sleeps with me
God sleeps with me.
My love knows me unto death all the way to the bottom
of a final fall.   For him I am
a vortex that doesn't stop
ripples ripples in the universe
I'll spray chills over ancient continents
I'll stiffen with pleasure the sea's soft down
I'll breed lizards with so much love
I'll cover the earth with searing flames
if not with pink babies
I'll unruffle the eiderdown of my love feathers
feathers into the sky
I'll refute gravity
split open my belly as you did
the wolf's.   Put stones in my belly!
but first let me
devour everything
with great voracity
with great voracity

The Fat Witch's Blues

I exchange kisses with chocolate
I melt into myself in a sweet paste
sharp paradoxes aching edges
I apply a fattening comforting ointment
I pour into myself meal after meal
warm   padding   inviting
like the warm palm
of mother
eating and more eating protect
against an emaciated world   evil
making sure I become a witch ablaze
inside a tepid   safe fire
a slow   arousing burning
eating ensures I won't be pretty
laying a protective layer across the belly
a warm blanket upon a small girl   cold
a small girl exchanging kisses with chocolate
eager eager
an ancient tunnel
mashing sucking
a mouth that sucks like a tunnel
swallowing stowing
protecting and shielding
so I'll be ugly   protected from love
systematically swelling up
so I can absorb the kick
so I won't be good enough
to lay
laying a large hand upon me   comforting
a thick horny blanket

inside a placenta to be swallowed inside
my mama inside
myself
to be my own pregnancy
to swallow me

Witch Discusses the Color Scale

Black is the lightest
of all colors
black is as clear as subconscious
waters

In the lower folds of my body there are dark masses
that have yet to be named
in your anemic
color scale

True darkness shines brighter
than the sun

From *Portrait of Mother and Daughter* (2010)

WEAVING

How do you weave together that which
is woven already?
The fear of death that squats inside me
like a beast
the exquisite morning   the beaming toddler across the way
    the worry accelerating
my wheels with a powerful engine   to worry   to worry
to remove from their path
any hurdle   I remove one   a new hurdle drops
a stone   I remove it   a new one drops
the mad race from here to there
my donkey-self taking on burdens
satchels   valises   bags laden with stones
flickering images of the faces
of my loved ones   a misery sprayed with shards of possible
joy   in spite of all
the music of weighty responsibility   trombones and basses
like a mute piano sitting on top of me
and I try
to haul it
up the stairs
and all the music shards are plaited together
in a delicate plait
invisible to me
a torn plait   tearing
glowing

A Small Prayer

God the Lord   creator of the universe
Please keep watch over
Those you've created
Keep watch over your world
Please do not keep yourself away from it
Please creator of all   supreme to all
Please do not keep yourself away from those you've made
From your wondrous world
Be good
Beneficent God
Be with us
Keep watch over yourself

SCAR TISSUE

At first I longed
for scar tissue. Let the hole
be covered.
Let the incision   heal.
Let the wound
close.

Everything was still
agape   gaping.
Slowly   the quiet of the closure
the hum of the binding
became audible
slowly slowly filament upon filament formed
the soft layers
of scar tissue

Slowly   it grew thicker
took on the hide of a tiny elephant
yes,   at first that of a sweet elephant cub   pinkish
slowly it grew   the skin grew thick
wooden   gray   slowly it grew   became stronger
slowly   the scar grew
in height
depth
width   outward   inward

Now it is me

Ejection Seat

I sit upon
my erratic ejection seat that flies
like an old broom
into giant clouds racing in a fast-motion camera

I'm hurled
upon an ejected ejection seat
falling
tracing the polygraph
of my chaos

LIFE AS AN ENORMOUS BEAST

Life as an enormous beast that sits on you
an enormous dark beast the size of a mountain
sits on you
and nibbles on you
calmly
satisfies her deep hunger
licks the blood off her lips

And you
underneath her
crushed   silent
slowly
devoured

SHE

From day to day she loses her strength
more and more she hangs onto me
she is wonderful and beautiful and dear to me
so much it hurts
and I cleave to her   adhere to her
and my soul is bound with hers in a thick braid
and now I run from her for a spell to a nearby café
to—what?

And outside   families with sweet kids in the holiday
and sweet cakes in the holiday   and a glorious sun in the
      holiday
and I try to get away from her
on this bright holiday
and presently I'll run back and be near her

And a world falls into a war pit
as I gather scraps of some trivial thin   thought
and inject it into this thin pen
as if it held some trace
of healing

And there's a lie   a lie   a lie
in every act of writing

BACK YARD

This morning, I took a back street off Ibn Gabirol* on my
     harried
breathless way to the café for a short break.
Her sadness. The back and forth between images of the
     abyss getting closer
and closer yet leaping from every corner gaping jaws
     grasping
paws—and between trying to take in the frail fragile
graceful pulsating things. To trust the beauty of her face
the beauty of her body of her wisdom of her poems
and not to be easy prey to the monsters
of the predictable script. To resuscitate mouth-to-mouth
to breathe more and more life and not to kill and not to
     murder
with idle** mouth and imagining.

I went past the back yard of a building, with its dusty
pine trees straining and the neglected shrubbery innocent
and the beauty hidden there. And something stirred in me
aching. As if all the dreams and the lively efforts of people
get shoved into their back yards into
the tool sheds the junk piles the garbage dumps

---

* A main thoroughfare in Tel Aviv, named after the medieval poet Solomon ibn
Gabirol.

** In the original—hevel: vanity, steam, vapor. "Vanity of vanities, saith the Preacher,
vanity of vanities, all is vanity." (Eccl. 1, 2).

In the Tiny Speck

Trying to divert my mind for a moment
I read something about the fact
that on the cosmic scale
our galaxy
is a tiny speck ---

In my tiny speck
the measure of the catastrophe extends
to cosmic scales

The sorrow zooms up to *Proxima Centauri*—
the neighboring star
the closest the closest—
a distance of four years of darkness and four more years of
    blackness

My pain over my mother
collapses into me
like a red dwarf

I play with the galaxy map
to allay

FROM THE NOTEBOOK

2/9/2002

The situation has deteriorated in a frightening way . . . new
problems . . . I tried to get nurses to come over.   I called.
I waited.   No one came over.   Only next morning a
caregiver arrived to help me . . . how she suffers . . .

2/11/2002

During calm moments, Mother expresses great love.

Tonight Chaim tells me that Mother said to him:
"People are strange. It's hard for them to be alone. And it's
hard for them with others."

And Chaim tells me that Mother said to him:
"If you're looking for something—look in the mirror."

MOTHER

Years upon years you take leave of your life
with extended hands   torn   you hold on
let go   hold on
years upon years   your eyes
brilliant still   your eyes grow dim   your eyes
not your eyes   your beauty alone
remains constant through all that infiltrates   your beauty
    alone
and she so alone   you so alone   she you alone
and how can I   sitting so securely in a chair
strapped in infinite security belts
how can I truly extend a hand to you   as the shrubs across the
    road
now extend toward me thousands of small blossoms
yellow   bold   young   and in the middle   a stream
of cars racing to their destinations
how can I   in this powerful stream   offer you
succor

And now on my heart sits a piano   heavy
not playing

My First Dream about You

My first dream about you
after you passed:
I dreamt last night that you're trying to commit suicide
swiftly seating yourself on the windowsill
in your room and—hop!—your entire body is in the air
except for your hands that somehow   (backward?)   hold
onto the sill.   And I try
to drag   to hoist   to save you—and succeed   (unlike real life
where gravity
dropped you me)

Later   after you've been saved and you sit or stand with me
you're asking for help   encouragement
someone to say with you that all will be all right   blessed be
      He
just as I've tried again and again to say with you
and how you joined me willingly faithfully

How you're alive and dead at the same time
flickering this way and that beyond your image, beyond the
      scenes
of my everyday life, beyond the cake that I devour,
astonished at myself for enjoying life so much   a life left to
      me alone

And here you are after all
full-
bodied   as soul-vapor only
and how I cling to you   reaching my arms to enfold you

The Neighborhood Cats, And Also the Birds

a recaptured photograph

How for decades you fed
all the neighborhood cats.
And all the birds, too.
You'd go to the butcher and buy meat for the cats
and for the birds you'd place water and seeds on the balcony.
Every day you'd go down to the yard and prepare a royal
cat-feast, even as the neighbors screamed   threatened
threw stones at the cats
threatened to stone you.
And how you recognized each cat according to its character
      and habits.
And when you couldn't go downstairs   you'd toss food for
      them
from the balcony.
Once as I came home
I counted more than thirty cats   a congregation
their faces upward   waiting for you as if for
God.
And you never discriminated between cat   and cat
between bird   and bird. And you found great beauty and
      wisdom
also in the crows.
And how they loved you

SOMEONE WENT PAST

Just now someone went past in the street—I know her—
hand in hand with her mother.   That someone is my age
and her mother is your age—and you could have been living
now hand in hand with me on the street

And my body recalls the light touch of your arm
as you leaned on me
a few days before your second fall—
when we walked to the synagogue   where Daddi's
bar-mitzvah was to take place
in a few days

And we walked in the street   on a wintry evening in February
    1996
and you said to me   "I feel so good running around with you
    like this"
and I was glad and we were loving

And then the accident   (the second)   the fall   the hip
and at the bar-mitzvah   when all of us celebrated in the
    synagogue
(with father ill)   you in hospital
broken   after surgery   bereft of your radiant joy

And later
with supreme effort
you were on your feet again

And we walked
hand in hand arm in arm

Until you were taken

AND NOW

And now   as the day's noise has ended
I'm left with only
the sighs of the dead of the night

Now   as the back-and-forth rushing is over with
and all the hankerings of the tumultuous day have stopped
I am only in the music
of my loved ones who are gone
who remain only in the hushed tone
in the whisper of the shut mouth   of those
whose mouths were locked by death
for good

Now   as the roar of the day has stopped   the roar
of the waves crashing in the world and against the world—
now   as I desist and lie down
having switched off all my cravings
I can hear the voices
of my mother   and father
weeping

Afterword

Raquel Chalfi and the Independence of Hebrew Women's Poetry

I

Hebrew women's poetry was born late and under revolutionary circumstances. Not before the 1920s could a group of women poets find its place in the Hebrew literary scene, and that only in the nascent Soviet Union (where poets such as Elisheva Bichovsky and Yocheved Bat Miryam emerged) and in Palestine (poets such as Esther Raab and Rachel Blovshteyn) of the era of the third *Aliya*, where the winds of Zionist utopian pioneering were reinforced by those of the Russian October. Hebrew women's poetry could be born then because the new revolutionary ethos, allowing for the liberation of suppressed cultural minorities, partly removed the restrictions that, until then, had all but eliminated the possibility of women's poetic self-expression to be accepted as "genuine" Hebrew poetry, i.e., as poetry based on the presuppositions that had informed the poetic practice of the turn-of-the-century Hebraic paragon H. N. Bialik and his many disciples.*

Of these restrictions, the demand for "rich," multilayered Hebrew, replete with subtle references to the sacrosanct "sources" (Bible,

---

* In the framework of this essay, I sometimes refer to, and quote from, poems (by Chalfi and others) that are not included in this collection. In such instances, the translation is mine. — D. M.

Talmud, Midrash, etc.)—and thus unavailable to Jewish women, whose education, whether traditional or modern, did not expose them to these sources—was only the most obvious one. It was only the upper tip of a larger ideological construct, which understood Modern Hebrew literature, and particularly its dominant genre, lyrical poetry, as a quest for the mental birth of a new Jewish subject out of the womb of traditional collectivist Judaism. This nascent subject and the travails he underwent throughout the process of being reborn as a modern individual had to be suffused with the culture and language of the past, those consisting, so to speak, of the placenta that had fed him but from which he had now to extricate himself. Women played no part in this drama of modernism overcoming tradition except as objects of a man's feelings and libidinous urges—in themselves indications of a new subjectivity grasping for self-assertion. Women's place in society, as well as their own quest for female subjectivity (as seen by men), were often dealt with by writers of prose fiction; there even emerged a single important Hebrew woman writer of fiction (Deborah Baron). However, the intensive expressivity and highly charged semantic messages ascribed to Hebrew poetic language were regarded as barriers no women could surmount. Jewish women poets were supposed to write their poetry, if at all, in languages other than Hebrew, such as Yiddish and Russian, which they actually did.

In the 1920s, as part of a general reshuffling of poetic priorities in Hebrew writing and the erosion of the dominance of Bialikian norms, the gates were thrown open, at least to a considerable extent. Among other liberating factors was the quick proliferation of Hebrew as it was now spoken in Palestine. As the avowed desideratum of Zionist cultural politics—the transformation of Hebrew from a literary to a spoken idiom—the "poor" spoken Hebrew of the new Palestinian community of pioneers and immigrants, devoid as it was of rich literary resonance, gained respectability, and was allowed to influence literary language in both Palestine and the Diaspora. Women poets made full use of this lowering of the linguistic bar. Some of them (particularly Rachel Blovshteyn) were among the first to elicit from the spoken Palestinian idiom its inherent musicality.

Once Hebrew women poets emerged in the 1920s, their cultural and linguistic "poverty" being now tolerated, they had to find their place along or vis-à-vis the male-dominated poetic mainstream. They were supposed to express female sensibilities (such as the more modest forms of female eroticism, the happiness of being loved by a man and the pain of unrequited heterogeneous love, the joys of motherhood and the excruciating suffering caused by childlessness), if possible in "simple" and short poems, which did not challenge the reader intellectually or culturally. Eventually the more talented of them managed to circumvent these limitations through irony (Rachel Blovshteyn) or rebellious emotional self-assertion (as in the expressionistic poems of Esther Raab and young Bat Miryam). Eventually they even managed to penetrate the citadel of intellectual reflection (particularly in the poetry of Lea Goldberg). Their project gathered momentum throughout the 1930s only to be enfeebled in the 1940s and early 1950s by the stormy atmosphere of war and struggle for Jewish survival in Europe and Palestine, which once again rendered male sensibilities—particularly those of men under fire, fighting for the existence of their community—the fulcrum of the zeitgeist. By and large, until the establishment of the state of Israel and half a decade into its history, women's presence in Hebrew poetry remained a sideshow, and was seen as complementary to the mainstream rather than as laying the foundations for a separate, independent tradition.

This changed as the new Israeli literary culture coalesced throughout the late 1950s and particularly the 1960s. Once the heady atmosphere of war, victory, and the ritual eulogizing of the fallen gradually abated and a rather mundane and often gloomy perception of reality replaced it, women poets' voice could again be clearly heard. Hebrew women's poetry was reborn, harboring new potential that would eventually endow it with a status it had never enjoyed before. This could be intuited already in the late 1950s from the light shed by the meteoric rise of the brilliant poet Dahlia Ravikovitch, every bit as talented and in possession of an authoritative poetic voice as any of her chief male contemporaries, Yehuda Amichai, Nathan Zach, and David Avidan. In the 1960s and 1970s, Ravikovitch's upsurge created a living space that was soon populated by a new generation of women poets, such as Dahlia Hertz, Nurit Zarhi, Hedva Harechavi, Yona Wallach, Raquel Chalfi, Agi Mishol, Maya Bejarano, Hammutal Bar-Yosef, and many others. Some of the older women poets, whose voice had been hushed throughout the

1940s, such as Zelda Shneurson and veteran Esther Raab, also regained volume. Hebrew, or rather Israeli, women's poetry was becoming what it actually is at the present: a poetic domain in its own right, very much in step with its male counterpart, and yet retaining full independence as a separate construct, which, while fully sharing with its counterpart the common components of Israeli literary culture, nevertheless processed them in its own manner.

This was achieved through a consistent, if usually undemonstrative, challenging by women poets of the dominant men poets' understanding of reality. Already in the 1950s Ravikovitch refrained from following any of her contemporaries' insights into the etiology of suffering in a world from which "mercy" was thoroughly emptied (Amichai). To Amichai this moral vacuity was the result of history as such, an ominous extrinsic entity always about to pounce and snatch the crumbs of happiness one managed to hoard in the closed but never sufficiently protected space of sexual intimacy. To Zach a pervasive malaise was mainly the result of an epistemological impasse: one could never "know" the truth about oneself or about the other. Always confronted by bad faith, wishful rationalizations and egotistic obtuseness, one's object relations were fragile as much as they were based on sheer projection. Even one's feeling of loneliness was spacious and misleading. Avidan's understanding of reality was inherently tragic due to the irresolvable clash between one's inherent self-image as a supremely dynamic and forceful subject and the objective existential reality of physical and mental decline and eventual death. Ravikovitch presented an altogether different version of suffering and mental pain, which emanated from a fractured ego always in flight from itself toward ever more fantastic and colorful landscapes of escapism, but also always recoiling from fantasy back toward the reality of an excruciating psychic pain. In her poetry the gray malaise spread over much of the writing of her contemporaries was forcefully swept off and replaced by the brilliant colorful binaries of the bipolar condition. The difference asserted itself through the style and the form, the haunting melos, the assertive rhythms and the rich figurative texture of her poems. The challenging of the dominant mood in early Israeli poetry was further developed and radicalized by women poets who soon joined

Ravikovitch, each of them, of course, conducting it in her own idio-syncratic manner. Raquel Chalfi's was one of the more interesting and productive among these new "feminine" interpreters of the real.

2

From the very start, in her early collections containing poems written in the 1960s and the 1970s, Chalfi formulated a poetic statement that went against the grain of the then dominant poetics; a statement calling for deflecting attention from the existentialist preoccupation with death, finality, bad faith, and the absurd aspects of the human condition, and focusing on the place of human existence within the wider framework of a universe awash with elemental energies, ceaselessly recreating itself through mobility and reiteration. Chalfi called directly and indirectly for a certain self-liberation through immersion in the living world rather than recoiling from it, through embracing the fleeting moment and be-coming attentive to whatever existed in the "margins" rather than in the "center," i.e., the domain of the broad entities, such as "life," "charac-ter," "choice," "truth" and all other components of existentialist phe-nomenology and ethics. In the face of all these abstractions, she flaunted reality in its minutest physical and emotional particles. She called for coordination between the human condition and the reality of physics and chemistry, for harmony with the world and its inexorable processes, and thus for a mood that did not preclude the option of ecstasy to the point of self-forgetfulness. All these were completely alien to the Israeli poetry of the 1950s and 1960s. Indeed, these epiphanies were exactly what that poetry warned against and repudiated.

In her first collection, *Underwater Poems and Other Poems,* pub-lished in 1975 (many of the poems were written in the 1960s), Chalfi included a few poems dealing with the experience of drowning ("The Sea Cellar," "Plucked Out"). In none of them does the experience entail fright and convulsion. On the contrary, the poems explore the silky in-side of water, whose outward surface is described as "hard as the mantle of a statue." The reader is invited to descend on an escalator of chiar-oscuro down to the sea cellar, where he will find nothing but "yearning darkness." The drowned woman in "Plucked Out" is projected as "dancing with corals, singing with the algae," asserting the "infinity" of water, which renders it the very opposite of death, grave, and tombstone. The poems, as indeed the entire "Underwater" cycle of which they are part, convey neither a neurotic death wish nor a facile aesthetic playing with one. Rather they form a metaphorical call on the part of the poet for the opening of one's consciousness toward whatever is flowing, deep, unstructured, and liminal. One is called to the task of "tying water with water" ("To Tie Water"), of "kneading darkness" into an ephemeral but palpable reality. One's teacher is to be the "Sculptor Fish," who knows how to treat the "hardest material," water, and with a slight, elegant flip of a fin or a tail "sculpt" it into a momentary, immediately perishable sculpture. This is also the mission of the poet: not to permanently "freeze" the mobile and unstructured real, but to endow it with perceivable albeit ephemeral and perishable formations.

This metaphorical call, as much as it triggers the vivid imagery of Chalfi's early poems (dealing mainly with various sea creatures and deceivingly sculpturesque flowers), amounts in fact to a cultural manifesto. The poet squarely positions herself in opposition to a pervasive cultural reductionism based on fear of the changing, always in flux, nature of reality and identifying it as the source of man's undoing, as well as on a lingering distrust with regard to everything that is not palpably "real," and epistemologically identifiable—a reductionism that expressed a generational recoiling from the Zionist ideal of self-denial and sacrifice softened by the vague promises of "life in death" or even life beyond death. "Plucked Out," for instance, directly deconstructs poems such as Amichai's early "The Woman Walked Away," in which the sight of a drowning woman initiates the poet's awareness of the thinness and fragility of his own "wall" of flesh, which separates "the sweet memories inside me from the big, salty world." Whereas to Amichai the outside world was not only "salty" but also ominous and invasive, Chalfi demands a recognition of the outside world as an extension of our interiority, or, vice versa, a recognition of our interiority's being a mere extension of an infinite and perpetually changing outside world. Amichai's position was based on the male experience of war and the vulnerability of the body. In contradistinction, Chalfi's position, while far from calling for renewed heroics and sacrifice of life, is based on a "feminine" sense of life's infinitude and flexibility. Hers is a call against living under the shadow of fear, and thus isolating oneself from the full awareness of being alive in the given moment, which is both fleeting and eternal. For the fish in the water nothing is "before" or "after." As much as the sculpting of the water is futile, it is also permanent in the sense that consciousness is unaware of any given moment in which it is not attempted.

Chalfi could be deemed a "feminist" poet to the extent that the concept of feminism is understood in epistemological rather than social and ethical-political terms. She is relatively uninterested in the roles a male-dominated society metes out to women, in imbalanced male-female dyads, in which women's sexual self-expression and intellectual freedom are tolerated only as long as their dependence on men is left unchallenged. Of course, she is aware of these and other injustices and instances of gender inequality, and makes them her focus in poems such as "From the Songs of Crazy Dolores," or the Bluebeard sequel, and the Witches cycle. However, in the best of these poems gender imbalances and inequality resulting in aggression and victimhood serve only as background for other, to Chalfi more disturbing, unresolved conflicts. Thus, for instance, she portrays Bluebeard, the proverbial egotist male, who exploits his many wives sexually and then—in Chalfi's version of the myth—does not kill but rather immures them alive in the walls of his palace, not so much as a sexual predator but rather as an emotional and intellectual coward (hence the color of his beard, the color of fear and depression), unable to stand up to the vitality of his wives, knowing himself "with every atom of his body" to be fragile and fearful, a weakling. He has to hide his wives in the walls because their presence undermines his shaky male potency, always confronting him with vitality far superior to his own.

At its core Chalfi's feminism is close to the philosophical-psychoanalytical feminism of thinkers such as Julia Kristeva rather than the social-combative tone of American feminist thinkers. It finds its full expression in poems such as "An Open Letter to Poetry Readers," one of the many declarative *Ars Poetica* poems Chalfi has written, in which she tells the story of the brain and its "little sister"—consciousness—(in Hebrew there are no neutral substantives and verbs; every noun, verb, and adjective must be gendered; thus the brain, *'mo'akh,'* is male, whereas consciousness, *'toda'ah,'* is female). The brain receives ten million cognitive events per second, of which "he" relays to consciousness only two or three. "He" performs this drastic act of reduction due to "his" loving and patronizingly protective attitude toward the "her" he envisages as little, young, and inexperienced. Being "wise" and "careful," he has taken upon himself to shield "her" against the uncontrolled barrage of impressions. Who knows if a less selective exposure would not have driven the "little" one to madness ("Keeps his little sister from going mad")?

This, of course, is based upon the little vignette in the last chapter of Solomon's Song, where a group of big brothers holds a council: "We have a little sister, and she hath no breasts; what shall we do for our sister in the day she shall be spoken for? If she be a wall we will build around her a palace of silver; and if she be a door, we will enclose her with boards of cedar" (8: 8–9). The poet, assuming the voice of the female speaker who rejects the brothers' protective "wisdom," ("I am a wall, and my breasts like towers" etc.), insists on making the need for a different relationship between the brain and the consciousness the topic of her poetry. Abstract and "nonpoetic" as this topic is, it is also of the essence. The poet could have written about more attractive themes, using flying, colorful, explosive metaphors, but she does not want to do that: "I can't. I can't want to" do this, she exclaims. She has to focus on the siege laid by the brain on consciousness. It is only by doing that that she can write at all. The readers want her to dwell on a green leaf and the emotions associated with its fragrance, but she feels the need to write about the space inside the leaf, "where minuscule currents transpire within the great pandemonium." They want her to display her physical and biographical profile rather than "the roar of boiling archeological layers" inside her, "the stirrings of the brief/ moment/where I am this one I facing that other I," i.e., where both "figure" and autobiography dissolve; but the poet refuses to either flaunt her feminine charms or share her life story with her readers. Rather she wants them to remember that "every bit travels ten million sound-light waves/ and its particles, infinitesimal photons impossible to imagine/ and even tinier quarks,/ explode in a lethal terrorist attack." Of course, what the poet wishes to convey in this and many other similar statements is not the scientific truth of nuclear physics. Her poems are replete with pseudoscientific lore, but it is always supposed to be understood metaphorically, representing the true nature of cognition rather than that of the physical world as such. It is this kind of cognition, organized by the "semiotic order" rather than by the "symbolic one," which she insists, as a woman poet, on introducing to Hebrew poetry. Of course, the "semiotic order," as discussed by Kristeva in her "La révolution du langage poétique," is feminine only at an abstract level, whereas in reality it can be practiced by men (such as the poet Lautréamont) as well as women, representing the feminine aspect of their cognition. By the same token, the Lacanian "Symbolic order," predicated on the centrality of the phallus, with the clear divisions it entails between the upper and lower, the flesh and the spirit, etc., can appeal to the masculine aspect of women's cognition and even constitute a kind of a subservient femininity. Thus Chalfi's feminism is and has been, from the very start, both impressionistic and philosophical. It is based upon her extraordinary ability to directly move from primary sensuous perceptivity to abstractions, bypassing many of the intermediary levels at which cognition is organized along narratives of moods, emotions, relationships and life story.

3

In her early collections, *Underwater Poems* (1975), *Free Fall* (1979), and *Chameleon or the Principle of Uncertainty* (1986), the poet evolved a fully-fledged poetics that allows for a systematic exploration of these principles and their ramifications. The poetics, no matter how complex and nuanced its textual realizations, supports itself upon four basic assumptions.

Number one: Chalfi systematically rejects all forms of perception to which she refers as "impositions." The category includes, as far as she is concerned, subcategories such as situation, character, plot, protagonist, meaning. All of these are seen as the "Will's backside," i.e., as the willful and heavy-handed misrepresentation of reality for the purpose of one's will. "Will's backside" crushes the Real underneath its massive preponderance, trying to suppress as mightily as it can the Real's staple characteristics: liminality and mobility. Thus the superimpositions under discussion eliminate, or at least drastically minimize, the exposure of one's consciousness to the truth of "the groping masses," the darting moments, the swirls of energy. To retain one's openness to all these, one has to train oneself in thinking "at the pace of darkness," to give up one's differentiation between the relevant and the irrelevant, the "important" and the "negligible." One has to turn one's attention toward whatever conventional selection jettisons and the cultural consensus despises. One's best teacher should be the chameleon, changing its color and complexion to merge with the environment. One should never accept reality "en bloc." Rather, one should feel and react to the dissimilarity hidden underneath all similarities, be able to breathe the "heavy air" as it spreads through the "clear air"; see the forms within the formless (such as water), the bright within the dark. By the same token, one has to regard one's own interiority as swarming with all kinds of unfamiliar entities. One has therefore to ceaselessly examine oneself, turn oneself into a petri dish, an aquarium, a pellucid glass container.

Number two: language as such amounts to an imposition, or a system of impositions, which the poet has to learn how to dexterously circumvent. It is ludicrous and pathetic in its futile attempt to "catch" and "freeze" parts of reality. In a series of *Ars Poetica* poems, Chalfi insists on the inadequacy of language. At best, words are "the sound of an owl at night," capturing a negligible fraction of the all-encompassing darkness, or amount to nothing more than the forlorn chirping of a gosling thrown out of its nest and into the abyss of the world. When employed with the purpose of freezing and captivating a piece of reality, they sometimes resemble lounge chairs on the beach flapping in the wind, unable to stop the swirling of sand grains, and at other times, large clumsy furniture with which one attempts in vain to halt a spinning floor. This view of language should not be seen as part of the distrust of language in general, and poetic Hebrew in particular—so typical of the canonical Hebrew poetry of the time—as it differs considerably from attitudes that may superficially look similar.

When Amichai defined himself as a poet who used "only a small part of the words in the dictionary," he pointed both to the remoteness and unsuitability of historical Hebrew as a vehicle for conveying current mundane experiences of real people, and to the deceptive and seductive power of "big" words, which can be manipulated and exploited by chauvinists and other demagogues. Chalfi is not particularly interested in this political and ideological abuse of language. She often uses both "big" words as well as mundane speech, mingling slang with literary language as long as both enhance the articulation of a tentative message, which approximates but never fully encapsulates the mental or physical reality it points to. Therefore her poetics abjure the meticulous search for the "right" or the "exact" word, and often favor modalities of redundancy. A poem to her is like a distant telephone call marred by atmospheric disturbances, and thus necessitating repetitions in similar or different words for the message to get through. Moreover, Chalfi often finds that too much linguistic concentration can mislead rather than direct. For instance, she writes (in her later collections) a series of poems about sitting in a noisy café, trying to shut her ears to the ongoing conversations around her, so that she can write her poem, only to discover that such a blockage is not only impossible but actually undesirable, since the conversations she overhears are as interesting and as important as anything she is trying to say in her poem. Thus she includes snippets of these conversations, slanderous and self-serving as they are, in the poem she eventually writes. Even the writing of a poem does not allow for a severance between the self and the clamorous world surrounding it.

Nathan Zach's distrust of language emanates from his assessment of the experience language is supposed to retain and, so to speak, eternalize as so fragile as to be reduced to "thin air" as soon as it is over. The assumption that the experience could somehow be preserved in words is delusional. How could a noun and adjective such as "pink evenings" retain anything of the mental reality of the "lost" experience of sunset? Chalfi's position is entirely different. Reality is never reduced to "thin air"; it is always as overwhelmingly rich and bountiful as it is shifty and evasive; so much so, that language is always chasing after it, never firmly grasping its magnificent tail. This, however, is not a reason for distrusting experience per se or for refusing to acknowledge the legitimacy of poetry. It is only an honest assessment of the "condition" and inherent shortcomings of linguistic expression, and as such a warning to the poet: he has to be constantly on the run; never delude himself into the belief that he has reached his final goal. If the goal is the conveyance of the sense of reality in its fullness, it can never be altogether accomplished.

Avidan, who of all his contemporaries entertained an almost mystical belief in the power of words, when properly used, to change reality, nevertheless bewailed their inability to bridge the gap between the subjective sense of exuberant life and the objective truth of impending decrepitude and death. He wrote: "Poems, as is their wont, divulge only what can be said in words, and therefore they throw themselves from the cliff to the great sea, where the breakers go up and down and down and up." Chalfi's answer to this could have been: By all means! Let the words, and the poems they add up to, throw themselves from the fixed cliff to the undulating waves, for that is exactly where they should be. And not out of despair of the power of words to retain youth and potency; the words and the poems should learn from the breakers the art of ceaseless mobility and thus give up on delusions of fixity and conservation.

Assumption number three: mobility, whether vertical or horizontal, is everything. From her earliest poems Chalfi explores mobility in its myriad modalities, starting with following the mobility of clouds over the seascape and ending with the cosmic centripetal spreading of space itself, where ever larger fanlike masses of particles are constantly contracting and opening up. In between, the poet closely watches various creatures in motion, people dancing the blues, the motility created by chemical reactions, witches shuttling through space, flowers folding and unfolding, and so on. In one of her earliest poems, which caught the imagination of readers, she follows "The Adventure of the Medusa Aurelia," which consists of the sea creature's rhythmical self-propelling—through constant absorption of water and its regular pumping out—from the dark depths of the sea toward the azure surface, where the sun eventually scorches it to death. Even when spread out on the hot beach sand, the medusa, as long as it is alive, rhythmically "dances," performing her wedding quadrille with her executioners: the light, the dryness, and the blue air that envelops it with "an asphyxiating bridal veil." In another early poem Chalfi practices mobility as a passenger in a bus on its way to Jerusalem on a moonlit night, teaching herself to experience the movement of the bus as progressively engulfing everything around it: "The window travels the clouds travel I/ travel the road travels the moon travels the trees travel the pane/ travels the moon travels the passengers travel/ the earth travels the mountains travel the planet travels the thoughts travel/ the time travels/ the light travels the glass travels the galaxy travels the moon travels" and only God is stationary. In yet another early poem, she presents life itself as "Freefall," the duration of which—from the moment of precipitation to the final crash—is that of life from birth to death. On her way from "the sky's chimneys" to "the land of my desires" (a parodist spoof on Zionist phraseology, and yet a genuine expression of love for earth in its fullness) the speaker encounters the angels bewailing her fall ("this is how it is in life"); she hears the voice of the inert stones, onto which she is about to drop, saying "long ago we too dropped with a bitter wail/ look at our this-is-it-*ness*/ and learn from us." Nevertheless, rather than buying into the Christian tragic myth of "the fall" (or of its secular-existentialist equivalent, *la chute*), she radically changes its significance. As long as the perpendicular movement is unstopped, she, the speaker, falls "eagerly." Freefall does not frighten her. Her scream is one of exhilaration rather than a wail; for movement is life, even if it is bound to end with a brief thud followed by endless inertia.

This equation of life with mobility leads Chalfi to a revolutionary understanding of space—rather than time—as the essential aspect of cognitive presence. For her space is an infinite ocean, whereas experienced time is just "the minnow of the minute," darting in its water. As for the historical past, it hardly exists in the early poems; or it does exist only to the extent that it has metamorphosed into a spatial entity, like historical Jerusalem which is not that different from the inert stones in "Freefall," waiting from time immemorial for the speaker to crash and be broken upon them. I call this kind of "chronotope"—where *topos* is everything and chronicity minuscule—"revolutionary" because in early Israeli poetry poetic space was drastically and intentionally shrunk in comparison with the place it had occupied in earlier Zionist literature, where the "conquest" of space was a cultural and an aesthetic desideratum, not devoid of political overtones. It was Amichai's and Zach's shared mission (in spite of all the differences between their respective poetics) to denude the space of a world totally devoid of mercy (see Amichai's "God Full of Mercy") of its shimmering mystique achieved through semireligious epiphanies, to devalue "place" and rootedness in it as a panacea. Instead, they emphasized the corrosive impact of time, which in the case of Amichai (but not that of Zach) could sometimes be mitigated by the renewal of love. Chalfi, of course, does not hanker back to the Zionist cult of reappropriated and redomesticated space. However, she definitely reaffirms the importance of epiphany as a source of knowledge, and uses her sense of space (as the appropriate arena for mobility, and therefore for genuine living) as a means for turning away from dominant mood and poetics in which she intuits a severe curtailment of the exhilaration of being fully alive. If her poetics can be described as feminist, it is her sense of space, perhaps more than anything else, which justifies such an appellation.

Assumption number four: The self or "central intelligence" of the poems, whether identified with the speaker or with a projected "she" (Dolores, Tutti, the witches, etc.), is never allowed to become a fixture. Like everything else, self is supposed to be in motion, to undergo metamorphoses, and even to become self-contradictory. In one of the early poems ("Suddenly") the speaker describes herself as an entity whose defining characteristic is the hectic rhythm of self-contradiction:

Suddenly I'm light suddenly I'm heavy
suddenly I'm round suddenly I'm sharp
suddenly I'm pretty suddenly I'm hideous
suddenly I'm open suddenly I'm clogged
suddenly I'm honest suddenly I'm crooked
suddenly I'm fat suddenly I'm skinny
suddenly I'm a doer suddenly I'm a dreamer

suddenly I love suddenly I don't love
suddenly I abstain suddenly I sleep around
suddenly I'm like this and suddenly I'm like that
suddenly I am I suddenly I
am not

This is not a call for irresponsibility and a rejection of consequential behavior. Rather it is a protest, in the name of psychological truth and intellectual integrity, against the autobiographism of early Israeli poetry, which in its rejection of Zionist collectivism projected the individual "I" as the steady basis for reported experience and thought, vouchsafing the "authenticity" of both the poem's contents and its articulation. Another prominent poet of the early Israeli decades, Dan Pagis, a Holocaust survivor, attacked these premises (which were so central to the influential poetics of Yehuda Amichai) in the name of those who were denuded by history of a real autobiography and a fixed identity, those who had been already dead but were somehow called back to life without being offered a new psychological birth (see his poem "Footprints"). Raquel Chalfi rejected the same premises in the name of the abundance of life and the promise of an almost momentary new psychological birth being always accessible to those who refuse to lock themselves in the prison of a rigid identity. That's why she believed at this stage that a poem could not really tell a story. With both the "world" at large and the "I" (or rather many, contradictory "I's") who observe and experience it, facing each other from positions which are never stationary, the poem could never assume the epic tone, which depends on the steadiness of at least one of the two components, mainly the "observer." For the young Chalfi, an authentic self, trying to function without imposing upon itself a reductivist control, could never become a mere "observer." She called for the removal of such "superimpositions," and tried her best at writing a poetry which was as free as possible from them. Of course, no poem can be completely free, since language itself is superimposed upon cognitive experience. The poet has therefore to try to use language with the intention of subverting its inherent tendency to superimpose, counting on repetition, semantic redundancy, alliteration, euphony, the intentional "warping" of grammar and syntax as well as other means that only an analysis of the poems in their original can identify and illustrate.

4

Whereas the assumptions we have just delineated remain to this day at the very center of Chalfi's poetics, later developments, starting with the collection *Matter* (1990), and achieving full swing in the poems of *Love of the Dragon* (1995), *A Hidden Passenger* (1999), and the collections that have appeared during the last decade, considerably qualify both their meaning and their practical application. One senses this as soon as one reads the first poems in *Matter*, particularly "Such Tenderness," one of the poet's best achievements, in which the hectic mobility of the earlier poems is consciously slowed down as the speaker records the slow process of aging:

> Such tenderness in our body
> as it abandons us
> slowly
> reluctant to hurt us
> with a sudden jolt.
> Gradually   wistfully
> like a half-sleeping beauty
> it weaves for us
> tiny wrinkles of light and wisdom—
> no earthquake cracks

Here, Chalfi's music is undergoing a change of register; her sense of time as an essential aspect of experience becomes suddenly so much more developed; her grammar and syntax, more "conventional" than they have been, conveying continuity and demanding a *legato* reading, rather than a *staccato* one. And yet, in principle, it is the same poet we meet here: the one accepting change as no reason for lugubrious existentialist moroseness, celebrating mobility, slow as it has become, finding beauty and grace in the folding and unfolding of the human body as it changes in preparation for death.

The poet now wrote a series of poems that could be described as self-deconstructive, i.e., poems in which the particular articulation in the earlier poems of motifs central to Chalfi's poetics is re-examined and importantly modified. As much as "Such Tenderness" could be understood as a "corrected" version of "Freefall," "Cubism," based on Picasso's Cubist portraiture, deconstructs Chalfi's earlier self-portraits as a writhing bundle of opposites. The Cubist approach allows for the continued presentation of the subject's face as consisting of irreconcilable parts. Yet, it nevertheless eventually yields a unified image by highlighting certain relationships between those parts, alien as they are to each other. Thus one's identity, being constructed of heterogeneous and even contradictory "I's," is not necessarily ruled by the *perpetuum mobile* which propels the early hectic poems with their ceaseless oscillating between the binary oppositions. Rather, it allows for slower and mellower procedures of relating those oppositions to each other. The speaker in "Cubism" points to the strange relationships between her "beautiful profile" and the "ugly" one to which it is glued. She feels that "the I that I was only a moment before laughs years ago," plays the role of the agile monkey in the jungle, in the face of the stiff-backed woman. Her answer to the question "which/ I is this   which I is that" was that all the "I's" crowded simultaneously "to cover up/ the mush/ of confusion."

In her new *Ars Poetica* poems (of which there are more than half a dozen), Chalfi revisits her quarrel with words and confirms her tendency to "reject" or push them away. But the confirmation includes important qualifications. Words are objectionable particularly when they are "light," devoid of some ponderous stuff, a "warm" mass which "connected them to something else." The poet cannot tell exactly of what that something consists, or where it can be found. It resembles some residue or deposit "not exactly in the belly not exactly in the earth, but somewhere beyond," that nevertheless sends arteries into the body. Once a connection with this residue is established, the words wake up and begin functioning, relating "chaos to chaos." ("A Quarrel")

In the long poem "The Theory of Poetry," the rapprochement with words moves one step further. A word (such as the Hebrew word *peten*, a snake) could function poetically if "suddenly" it struck the "memory cells," sweeping the "memory worms" into a crazy dance. Quoting an early poem of hers, Chalfi draws new conclusions from it. The short poem, now included in the much longer one, explains what semiotics is. "The theory of semiotics is the theory of scars. The theory of scars is a set of wounds that have not altogether healed." "A wound which healed is near-transparent, and who can talk in the language of transparencies; not even a glazier, let alone a semiotics expert." Thus the early poem explains why so often words are poetically dysfunctional: being transparent they connect too quickly and too fully the sign with the signified, leaving no superfluous semantic detritus behind them. However, now, in the late poem, the other possibility is explored. What if words, on their way from the sign to the signified, are detained, bumping into the opaque lump of a semantic scar and, in the process, tear their surface, spill some unused phonetic matter, become a bit dirty, carry beyond them some semantically nonfunctional trails? Then presumably they could undergo a rebirth of sorts and start to function poetically.

In this context of self-deconstruction, one late poem, "The Love of Trees," is particularly significant. It relates directly to one of Chalfi's strongest early poems, "Absalom's Terebinth." That poem is based on the biblical story about King David's favorite but disloyal son, who fomented a rebellion against his father and then was killed in battle. This happened when he was riding on his horse and his beautiful head of hair got entangled in the branches of a terebinth tree, leaving him hanging in the air, his bare chest an easy target for the enemy's lances. Chalfi interpreted the classical story (at the time, Yona Wallach did that, too, but in a totally different manner) as an example of the inherent unity of a world, in fierce motion, leading to collision. Mobility often leads in this world to horrific fusions, one moving thing losing itself in the mass of the other. In Chalfi's poem it is not only Absalom, frenetically fleeing his enemies, but also the stationary terebinth that experiences a similarly frenetic mobility. Even before the clash with the man takes place, the tree is throbbing, writhing from root to the tips of its boughs, in preparation for that clash. Its entire leafage is "horny" for the approaching young man. Absalom, in his turn, is undergoing a process of "timbering" or "lumbering" as soon as his hair is caught by the tree's tentacles. His long tresses become one with the tree's dark-green leafage, his arteries stiffen and his brain, now washed with the tree's pungent and viscous resin, goes crazy. The man and the tree present "a symbiosis of a male and a female tree."

In "The Love of Trees" the revisited theme of an erotic encounter between a human and a tree is treated with a sense of humor as well as a full awareness of the unbridgeable gap separating a living creature from the arboreal. Here it is the speaker, a woman, who tries to "seduce" the trees. As a person she lacks "an ancient calm" which she wishes to absorb from the vegetative world. She embraces the trees, holding her body tight to their "peaceful thick trunks," and as she rubs herself against them she enjoys their "simple roughness." Presumably, she gets herself into a semierotic trancelike state in which she wishes to induce the condition of fusion ("And bit by bit/ I/ am no/ longer I/ and gradually/ I am more and more/ I"). The poem ends, however, not with a celebration of this state of soporific intermingling, but rather with an abrupt awakening from it. The speaker, away from her favorite trees and back in her study, sitting "on a jittery chair" and trying to write a poem about her experience, sums it up, rather flippantly, with a bit of practical advice to her readers: "listen people:/ There's nothing like a quiet embrace with a large tree/ to chase away/ the demons." Thus the ideal of fusion has been reduced to a therapeutic technique; ecstatic epiphany is replaced by common, good-natured wisdom—wishing to share the experience with others—and the sudden invasion of the poem by listeners ("listen people") indicates that the previous union with the trees was never as intimate and quasiepiphanous as it pretended to be. From the start, the poet was standing in the public arena of literature and its readers.

5

Chalfi's late poetry can be said to have qualified the poet's core poetics in many ways. More important, perhaps, than all others is the change that takes place in object-relation as it is reflected in the poems. In her early work Chalfi hardly acknowledges the existence of a separate and quintessentially other. In her world of flowing energies, galactic mobility, fusions, and chemical reactions, the other, to the extent it shows up at all, is a radicalized self-image embodying the more dynamic components of the speaker's personality. Such are all the witches, most of the sea creatures and exotic flowers, Dolores, Tutti, and all the rest. Completely exceptional in this respect is the early long poem dedicated to the poet's primary-school teacher Sara, whose face and character are distinctly and lovingly (and yet also perspicaciously: the speaker realized as a child that the heavy makeup her beautiful teacher wore was meant to cover a mysterious scar) drawn in a manner that does not allow for projection of the self through the portrayal of the other. Now, starting in the late 1980s, such poems appear in progressively greater numbers. The poet is aware of herself and everybody else as being both similar but also totally dissimilar to all others. Indeed, she is as "alien" to all the rest as if she had just descended from a far-off star. In her poem "Aliens" she looks at the man or the woman facing her, thinking how much they are like her. "The hands, the legs, the eyes, the hair, the common human wretchedness, the few sparks of hope ignited in the darkness of that walking mass" are exactly the same. And yet how lost in his or her individuality everyone is, how "alien." Playing with the Hebrew word for alien in the science-fiction sense of the term, *Khaizar*, she breaks it into its two components: *khai*—a living creature, being alive—and *zar*—alien, being the other. Whereas life is the common denominator, being the other is where genuine object relation begins. Unless one sees a person as the other, one is unable "to save the person so that he would save oneself."

Gaining that insight could not be quick and easy. It involved a protracted process consisting of "crystalline moments," of tracing an "inter-galactic" truth as if through a telescope, because the distance otherness entailed was "inter-galactic." I believe the process began in a poem from the early 1990s about a friend who lost her sanity, irretrievably sinking into psychosis. The poem, defined as a "kina" (the ancient Hebrew genre of lamentation, a dirge), is charged with sharp emotions of grief and pained empathy, and is highly metaphorical, proceeding from one extreme metaphor to the other (the friend was a bunch of ""poppies breaking/under the weight of the tar of madness""; she was "a glowing insect/under a voracious beast in the dark"; her body was filled with "a warm" animal, which crushed it from the inside and the outside; she was finally engulfed, "frozen/ in the basalt" of the sane and clear awareness of her own impending devastation, etc.). However, she was not in any way or form a reflection of the speaker. As a matter of fact, the latter, watching from the outside the breakdown of her friend, did not really know what was going on in her mind and body. Out of empathy she made a huge effort to penetrate the other person's interiority, and the effort found its expression in the not altogether successful heaping of one big metaphor upon the other. Toward the end of the poem the speaker is honest enough to demarcate the distinction: the friend, the Job of the poem; she, the speaker, is only one of Job's friends.

Clearly the realization of the otherness of the other demanded effort on the part of Chalfi, but she progressively became more adept and successful in handling that effort. Writing many sequels of poems that could be described as exercises in the imaginative actualization and mental internalization of otherness, she now turned upside down a metaphor she had frequently used in her early poems, that of the aquarium or the glass receptacle. Whereas in the early poems the aquarium always represents the self, inside which strange creatures (unknown parts of one's psyche) live and uncontrollable processes (psychic changes) take place, now the glass wall, standing for distance and the transparency needed for close observation, marks the boundaries between the self and the other. These boundaries do not entail coldness, lack of emotion, sheer voyeurism. On the contrary, they are open to transports of empathy as well as to actual attempts at helping the suffering other. Nevertheless, they eliminate fusion, intermingling, and the circularity of self-love through the projected other.

These qualities of seeing the other for what he is, and yet striving for contact with him or her find their acute expression in the series of poems Chalfi dedicated to her parents, each of whom was an artist in his or her own right, in the wake of their demise, and to her son Daniel as he grew from a toddler to a strapping young man. But it is not only relatives and friends who now draw the poet's attention and sympathy. Strangers randomly met also become the recipients of warm-hearted relatedness. Thus Chalfi, who in her youth seemed to have been lost in storms of particles and geysers of energies, now becomes—without having lost her "cosmic" awareness—one of the more distinct voices of humanism in Israeli poetry. She could now use the formulae and rhythms of vacillating between oppositions as means for the articulation (in a poem titled "What Is") of a message such as:

> What is it to be depressed at the age of 20
> Compared to taking a shower at the age of 90.
> What is it to get into bed with a woman at the age of 21
> Compared to getting out of bed without a woman at 81.
> What is it to read poetry when one's 16
> Compared to getting one's foot into a shoe at 89. [...]
> What is it to get drunk at 30
> Compared to drinking without spilling water at 90.
> What is it to write a dissertation in Linguistics at 29
> Compared to getting a slip of paper [one needs] from the inane
>   clerk at 74.
> What is it to climb the Himalaya at 26
> Compared to boarding the bus at 86. [...]
> What is it to hover in meditation at 37
> Compared to standing in the bathtub at 97.
> What is it to have written this sitting at 40
> Compared to reading this lying at 90
> And then trying to get
> Up.

The poem just quoted (as well as other poems like "Such Tenderness") clearly points to a shift in the balance (or rather imbalance) of space/time in Chalfi's poetry. Her chronotope assumes, right before our eyes, a new form with the component of time occupying a much larger section than the tiny, needle-head one it had been once allowed to occupy. Even the digits used for indicating the difference between the ages and thus the passage of time are worthy now of entering the body of the poem.

Cosmic space still looms large in the poet's mind and imagination; but time, human time (which is the time measured by the duration of life), "penetrates" the body of the speaker as a solid substance, changes balances within it, sculpts changing face and torso, creates new continuities and discontinuities. In one poem ("At Two pm in Ein-Kerem") the speaker, listening to the bells of the many churches of this village near Jerusalem telling the hour, suddenly feels how time, having assumed an acoustic "materiality," penetrates her. Putting "flesh and skin and light" around its, until now, imperceptible body, it becomes "a creature humungous, caressable": "Suddenly time suddenly has a volume heavily breathing." The penetration "right into a dimension inside me" is quite painful, and the poem is replete with abrupt "ouches" and "eees." Nevertheless, the process is also pleasurable, like an unforeseen but welcome sexual penetration. The speaker at the end of the poem is filled with a presence in which time present (in Hebrew: *hove*) merges into the divine presence (in Hebrew: *Yahave*, the Ineffable Name), the merger bringing with it a strange, ponderous ecstasy. Thus time too assumes the shimmering form of an epiphany in Chalfi's poems.

This could not but impact space as well. Infinite and mobile as it ever was, it also becomes less turbulent. Mobility within it (as well as its own mobility) waxes slower. Being in it now feels like calm floating rather than hectic zooming or convulsive folding and unfolding (see the poem "Sub Matter," beginning with the verses: "I sail sail sail/ in the vast space of the sub-matter/ of my minutely minuscule life"). What's even more important, the poet's attention is now gradually turned from the vast ocean of space to its mundane shores, those of normal, daily human existence. This shift of attention from the vast to the "petty" is often felt as difficult but necessary. In the poem "Events at the Beach" the speaker asks herself: "The arms of the sea are wide enough to embrace more than half of the planet, so why should I ensconce myself in a narrow corner?" At the same time she knows that while absorbing herself mentally in the "ancient turquoise" splendor of the water, she is avoiding something important, glossing over a dangerous eddy, "cheating a bit." In order to touch the missed truth, she has to focus on a random person walking along the beach until reduced to a tiny dot; scrutinize a half torn-down building, in which an old man stands and then takes off his clothes; look at the single "serious raven, who was now descending towards the roof [of that building], trying to understand something." In another poem, "A Niche in Chaos," she discovers that the ethical imperative impacts the formation of space, bending it, forcing the person floating in the huge unfolding chaos to dig a small alcove or niche in it, to paint this niche in white, render it habitable, install drawers in it, and try to get as much of oneself as is possible into that niche.

Thus in Chalfi's late poetry space undergoes a process of relative shrinkage. Many of the poems' plots now take place among houses, trees, streets, coffeehouses (where the poet says she could temporarily extricate herself and her dark-adjacent mass "from fierce gravitation," penetrate a different space, assume a different mass, obey different laws of gravity ("Give me a Coffee House"), and also in the privacy of one's own home, an enclosure that is not presented as barrier between oneself and the world. Rather it becomes a steady, reliable base, for which the poet, after roaming far and wide in both outer and inner spaces, yearns, as she tells us in "Let Me Have a Bowl":

> let me sit in a chair
> lie on a bed
> walk on a sidewalk
> let me place a hand on
> a solid wood table
> rather than on a void dotted here and there
> with crumbs and shadows
> of particles of inscrutable energy.

In the Hebrew original the speaker wishes to sit "on" a chair, to lie "on" a bed; the word "solid" (*atum*) also conveys associations of something shut off, impermeable, impenetrable. Clearly, the poem gives vent to an accumulated fatigue or impatience with what is unfixed, unsupportive of weight, whatever one cannot lean on. Such impatience does not, of course, mean that reality suddenly becomes a safe haven for the floating consciousness. The poet knows only too well that the solidity she craves is imaginary, and that the reality of the world is that of an abyss. What has changed, though, is what one may call the élan of throwing oneself into the abyss. In her early poems, we remember, Chalfi found freefall desirable, no matter how harsh the final crash was going to be. Now her wishes have changed.

Together with them, her concept of the self has undergone a subtle metamorphosis. Still, it is fragmentary and self-contradictory, but as the poem "Cubism" suggests, it has become less fluid and formless. If it still is "a dangerous kaleidoscope," at least the colorful glass pieces that are jerked in it from side to side, always forming new patterns by being mirrored and duplicated, are solid enough. In many of the poems they are visibly, and comically, "glued" to one another as much as the speaker's beautiful profile is immovably glued to the ugly one. In one of her funniest poems the poet compares herself to the strange Australian ducklike creature called Paradoxus. Looking like a duckling, it was both a mammal and a bird, and a marine animal to boot. As a mammal it nevertheless laid eggs, but when its goslings hatched it lactated, feeding them from regular nipples to which they attached themselves with thick, hardened, wooden bills that made the sound of castanets. The Paradoxus was "a paradoxical duck" consisting of "amalgamated contradictions," and yet it was a living and functional creature, which managed, although with considerable difficulty, to "navigate through deep waters" and perpetuate its endangered species.

One is fluid, changeable, and flexible; but also necessarily hardened and, at times, frozen. This hardening is as essential for existence as are flexibility and malleability. For Chalfi, "Lot's Wife" is not the biblical figure of the woman who could not restrain herself when fleeing Sodom; the one who had to look back, in spite of divine warning, and therefore froze to a pillar of salt. Rather, every one of us, including the poet herself, has no choice but intermittently to play the role of Lot's wife, look back and temporarily freeze. As much as we yearn to be one with, and get lost in, the shimmering flux of flowing energies, we are constantly reined in by forces such as the "articulate" rational mind and the "victorious ego," memory and attachment. The speaker wishes to stay awhile with "the noise, the darkness, the diminishing light, the music, the vegetation, which can penetrate," but constantly has to cast and recast "this minuscule atom which is I" as a large plaster mask. There is no growing a self without such casting and recasting. Indeed, if we wish to live, we also have to create for ourselves temporary death masks.

༈

Chalfi's poetry keeps changing and evolving as it also remains rooted at its core perception of reality. In all its transformations and transfigurations, however, it is fiercely independent, conveying a strong ethos of loyalty to one's perception and experience. In her independence, which renders her so distinctly different from all other Hebrew poets, Chalfi nevertheless stands for femininity in the philosophical and epistemological rather than the biological, psychological, and sociological senses of the term. Thus her poetry is playing an important role in the refashioning of Israeli culture. What is feminine about her is the way she experiences space and time, and thus also the concepts of land and history so fiercely fought over by the contending factions that are and have been for the last fifty years at one other's throat in their struggle over the fashioning of Israel's cultural identity. Of course, she is also a woman who knows love and the pleasures of the body, and who is acutely attuned to the emotions pertaining to being a daughter and a mother. However, what is paramount in her feminist legacy is her call for perceptual and intellectual open-endedness. Whereas we more or less know how to activate our various organs, she teaches our brain how to function, perceive, process data, form judgments. No less than a poet, she is a thinker.

DAN MIRON
Columbia University, New York
April–May 2014

Acknowledgments

The following poems have appeared in the following publications:

American Poetry Review: "Such Tenderness," "Going Up and Down the Stairs"

Zoland Annual: "Reality Crumbs in Café Marsand"

Metamorphoses: "Cubism," "Tale about an Inside-Out Dress," "The Love of Trees"

Iodine Poetry Journal: "Signs"

Grey Sparrow Journal: "A Brief Love"

World Literature Today: "Double Exposure in the Black Forest"

The Collagist: "Laundry"

Gertrude Press: "Mutant Witch," "Witch in Fact"

The Posen Library of Jewish Culture and Civilization (New Haven: Yale University Press, 2013): "On the Shore, Tel Aviv, Winter 1974"

"Traveling to Jerusalem on a Moon Night," "Hair of Night," "The Water Queen of Jerusalem," "Reckless Love," "I Drew My End Near," "Sitting in the Wall," "Monologue of the Witch Impregnated by the Devil," "And the Whiteness Grew Stark," "Elegy for a Friend Who Lost Her Mind," "A Hidden Passenger," "Blues in a Jar," and "German Boot" previously appeared in *Poets on the Edge: An Anthology of Contemporary Hebrew Poetry* (Albany, NY: SUNY Press, 2008).

This project was made possible, in part, by a National Endowment for the Arts fellowship.

About Raquel Chalfi

Raquel Chalfi was born in Tel Aviv, where she lives and works. She studied at the Hebrew University, at the University of California at Berkeley, and at the American Film Institute. She worked for Israeli radio and television as a writer, director, and producer, and has taught film at Tel Aviv University. She has published fifteen volumes of poetry, as well as a collection of short stories. Her work has been translated into English, Arabic, French, Italian, German, Portuguese, and Spanish; a selection of her poems, *Cameleon*, was published in Belgium by L'Arbre à Paroles in 2008. She is the recipient of numerous awards for her poetry, and for her work in theater, radio, and film. Her collected poems, *Solar Plexus, Poems 1975–1999*, appeared in 2005, and in 2006 she received the prestigious Bialik Award for poetry, and the Brenner Award in 2013.

Poetry volumes published in Hebrew

Underwater Poems and Other Poems, Hakibbutz Hameuchad, 1975 [Shir-im Tat-Yami`im Ve-Aherim]

Freefall, Marcus/Achshav, 1979 [Nefilah Hofshit]

Chameleon or the Principle of Uncertainty, Hakibbutz Hameuchad, 1986 [Zikit O Ekron Ee-Ha-Vada`ut]

Matter, Hakibbutz Hameuchad, 1990 [Khomer]

Love of the Dragon, Hakibbutz Hameuchad, 1995 [Ahavat Ha-Drakon]

A Hidden Passenger, Hakibbutz Hameuchad, 1999 [Nosa`at Semuyah]
Solar Plexus: Poems 1975–1999, Hakibbutz Hameuchad, 2005 [Miklaat Ha-Shemesh]
Portrait of Father and Daughter, Keshev, 2004 [Tmuna Shel Abba Ve-Yalda]
Secret Details from the Transparent Portfolio, Hakibbutz Hameuchad, 2007 [Pratim Sodiim Mitoch Ha-Klaser Ha-Shakuf]
Witches, Keshev, 2009 [Mechshefot]
Portrait of Mother and Daughter, Keshev, 2010 [Tmuna Shel Ima Ve-Yalda]
Poems for Daniel, Keshev, 2011 [Shirim L'Daniel]
The Book of Creatures, Hakibbutz Hameuchad, 2011 [Sefer Ha-Yetsurim]
China, Hakibbutz Hameuchad, 2013 [Cin]
Margins, Hakibbutz Hameuchad, 2014 [Shula'yim]

PROSE

Blue Against the Evil Eye, Hakibbutz Hameuchad, 2012 [Kachol Neged Ayin Ha'ra]

BOOKS IN TRANSLATION

Cameleon, L'Arbre à Paroles (Belgium), 2008

AWARDS

2013—The Brenner Award for Poetry
2006—The Bialik Award for Poetry
2000—The Judges' Ashman Award for Literature, Akum
1999, 1989—The Prime Minister Award for Literature
1983, 1986—Film Awards—Israel Film Institute
1977—The "Ondas" International Award (Barcelona) for Best Documentary Radio Program
1977—The Israel Broadcasting Authority Award

1976—Best Feature Screenplay Award—National Council for Culture and the Arts

1976—Best Radio Documentary Award—The Israel Broadcasting Authority

1971—The Shubert Playwriting Award—The University of California at Berkeley

1967—Best Original Play Award—National Council for Culture and the Arts

About Tsipi Keller

The author of ten books, Tsipi Keller was born in Prague, raised in Israel, and has been living in the United States since 1974. She holds a graduate degree in English from New York University, and is the recipient of several literary awards, including National Endowment for the Arts Translation Fellowships, New York Foundation for the Arts fiction grants, and an Armand G. Erpf Translation Award from Columbia University. Her translation of Dan Pagis's posthumous collection *Last Poems* was published by The Quarterly Review of Literature (1993), and her translation of Irit Katzir's posthumous collection *And I Wrote Poems* was published by Carmel (2000). Her other translation collections include: *Poets on the Edge: An Anthology of Contemporary Hebrew Poetry* (SUNY Press, 2008); and *The Hymns of Job & Other Poems* (A Lannan Translation Selection, BOA Editions, 2008). Her novel *The Prophet of Tenth Street* was published by SUNY Press in 2012, and her selected volume of Erez Bitton's poems, *You Who Cross My Path*, is forthcoming from BOA Editions.

About Dan Miron

Dan Miron (b. 1934) was born and raised in Tel Aviv. He received his education in Jerusalem (The Hebrew University of Jerusalem, The Rubin Academy of Music). Since 1953 he has published many hundreds of literary-critical essays and articles and about fifty books of literary scholarship. He has also edited the variorum editions of the works of some of the greatest Hebrew writers, such as the poets H. N. Bialik and U. Z. Greenberg. He is widely regarded as the leading authority in the historical interpretation of modern Jewish literature (particularly its Hebrew and Yiddish branches) and as an influential critic of Israeli literature. Having taught at the Hebrew University and the University of Tel Aviv, he was nominated in 1987 to be the holder of the Leonard Kaye Chair of Hebrew and Comparative Literature at Columbia University in New York. His books have been published in Hebrew, Yiddish, English, German, and Russian. A recent publication in English is the magisterial *From Continuity to Contiguity—Toward a New Jewish Literary Thinking* (Stanford University Press, 2010), for which he won the National Jewish Book Award in the field of Jewish scholarship.

Index of Titles and First Lines

A Brief Love, 8

A Half-Day Off, 140

A Hat's Architecture, 55

A Hidden Passenger, 60

A Moment in the Inner Glass, 76

A Moment Tries to Catch Itself by
Its Tail, 144

A Sex-Mechanic in Berkeley, 25

A Small Prayer, 176

A Witch Bent on Healing, 161

An Open Letter to Poetry Readers,
42

And How You're Trying To Make Me
Laugh, 120

And Now, 188

And now what?, 72

And the Whiteness Grew Stark, 29

Ants, 133

Back Yard, 181

Bear Song, 58

Birthmark, 77

Blues in a Jar, 61

Busy, 69

Chameleon, 23

Cinema, 146

Cubism, 78

Daily Record, 21

Dissolves, 44

Don't Tell Me, 137

Double Exposure in the Black
Forest, 138

Ejection Seat, 178

Elegy for a Friend Who Lost Her
Mind, 56

Eurydice, 70

Father Who Comes and Appears, 124

For, 19

Freefall, 14

From the Diary of a Penguinette, 152

From the Notebook, 183

From the Songs of Crazy Dolores, 4

German Boot, 85

Going Up and Down the Stairs, 27

Greenhouse Effect, 102

Hair of Night, 12

Handling Pain, 20

Here   in the Hidden House, 131

Hopeful Witch, 166

I Drew My End Near, 18

I'm Sitting, 119

I Put Over My Head, 118

I Went to Work as an Ostrich, 46

If Only I Were a Fearless Biker, 147

In Such a Furnace of Noon, 134

In the Tiny Speck, 182

Internal Gymnastics, 92

Laundry, 110

Let Me Have a Bowl, 101

Life as an Enormous Beast, 179

Love at McDonald's, 142

Metaphors, 130

Monologue of the Witch
    Impregnated by the Devil, 168

More and More They Wrap, 128

Mother, 184

Mrs. Darwin, 156

Mutant Witch, 163

My First Dream about You, 185

Nearly, 113

Niche, 24

On the Shore, Tel Aviv, Winter
    1974, 11

Once I Knew, 53

Optimism in an English Meadow, 31

Organism,   Chaos, 99

Parrot in My Brain, 59

Pictures from a Diary, 105

Poem about Sky, Stone, Sea, 40

Reality Crumbs in Café Marsand, 62

Reckless Love, 16

Relationship, 2, 45

Scanner, 79

Scar Tissue, 177

She, 180

Short Ones, 150

Signs, 48

Sitting in the Wall, 26

Sixty-Five Million Years Ago, 149

So Why Don't I, 136

Someone Went Past, 187

Sometimes   At Noon, 68

Space Pockets, 108

Sub-Matter, 94

Such Tenderness, 54

Suckling, 114

Suddenly, 41

Tale about an Inside-Out Dress, 57

The Cat Frasier as a Philosophy
    Major, 143

The Cute Word-Strollers, 127

The Fat Witch's Blues, 169

The Glow of the Child, 104

The Love of Trees, 81

The Magical Cat, 28

The Neighborhood Cats, And Also
    the Birds 186

The Objects, 112

The Soul or Possibly, 75